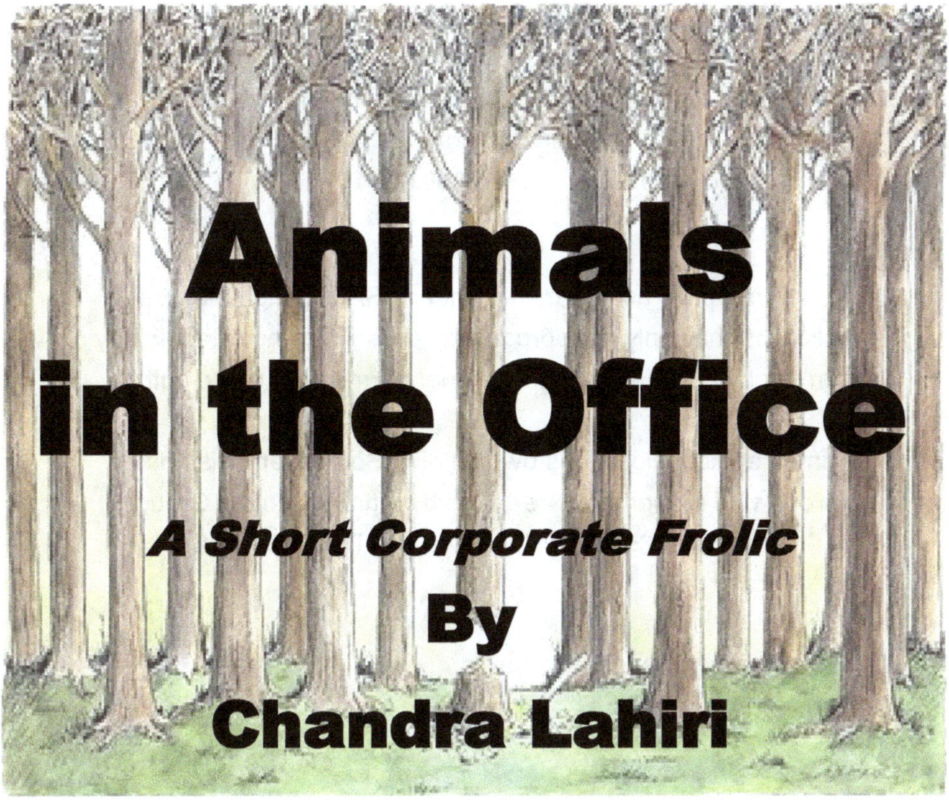

Animals in the Office

A Short Corporate Frolic

By

Chandra Lahiri

First Edition : 2012
Second Edition : 2024
ISBN : 979-8-8691-8716-1

Printed at global locations by Lightning Source, and distributed worldwide (paperback & e-book) by Ingram Content Group, One Ingram Boulevard, La Vergne, TN 37086, U.S.A

DAWN VOYAGER

CONTENTS

Chapter 1

Donkey & Owl

Donkey was having a bad day – I mean, a *really* bad day. A quarrelsome queue of animals had built up outside his door, trying to jump over each other to get in, to see him, with all their trivial problems. For some reason, all the animals expected 'decisions' from him. No one seemed to realize he had a terrible headache and that, above all, even the thought of having to make a decision simply petrified his simple little donkey brain. After all, he had successfully built an entire career by seeming decisive, but actually avoiding even a statement that could be construed as any sort of commitment. Long ago, he had realized that the key to success in this Lion's Forest was to ensure no blame could ever be pinned on you. No wonder he had never made any mistakes, never upset anyone and, with his Colgate smile and sunny donkey personality, had risen to the top of the heap, as Chief Executive Animal, or CEA, of his corporate Sanctuary, at a remarkably young age. In a Forest nation full of predators, he had skillfully kept his hide intact, and made friends with all the media birds who twittered his praises all over this neck of the woods. It had been hard work trying to pull the wool over all the animals' eyes - but he had succeeded. And here he was now, CEA of one of the most important Sanctuaries in this Forest. It had been easy to bolster his self-belief by the simple expedient of not listening to anyone with a contrary view. And here were all his little animals disturbing his peace, and actually expecting him to stick his very precious donkey neck out, by taking decisions! The cheek of it all! After all he had done for them, ensuring they had warm little burrows, plenty of juicy snacks, lots of holidays to laze in the winter sun, and absolutely no thinking of any sort to do. Surely he deserved a little gratitude. And to make matters worse, most of the Asses on his Board of Director Animals were also braying for various actions and accountability from him. Between them, poor CEA Donkey was having a very bad day.

Dove, his long-suffering Secretarimal, peeped in timidly, and gently chirped a reminder about his meeting with Owl, in the Forest Clearing Den. This had the effect of a hard kick to Donkey's rear, sending a shock of pain to his already hurting little brain. He had blissfully forgotten all about pesky Owl. Donkey had managed to avoid meeting him so many times, with a really ingenious variety of excuses, ranging from Owl's waking hours not coinciding with his own to (very frequently) simply escaping on an aimless jaunt to foreign Forests. Now, wretched Owl had finally cornered him, and seemed to be in deadly earnest about a decision on his pet beach bird-bath project. He seemed to have no appreciation for the fact that Donkey just did not make decisions – at any cost. What made it worse was the fact that, away from the office, Owl was a friend...of sorts. Of all animals, he should have had some consideration for the over-taxed brain of poor Donkey.

Unable to escape the inevitable, he ambled off into the Forest, taking his time to sample tempting fruit here and a bit of luscious grass there, stopping to admire the sunbeams shining through the trees. His very relaxed waking daze was suddenly interrupted by a chirpy chirrup from the branch above him. "Hi, CEA Donkey!" trilled a media bird.

"Oh, hi, Twit", responded Donkey cheerfully, immediately switching on his high-wattage smile and benign look, "My, aren't you looking especially lovely this morning?"

"Thank you, kind sir. We missed you at our last corporate party," said Twit, batting her long eyelashes, as usual.

"Ah, I was away, travelling in the Sunset Lands. As you know, I have a really hard life – I have to travel almost three weeks in every month, to one distant Forest or the other. There is simply so much work to be done, with the huge number of projects King Lion's Minister has entrusted me with," said Donkey.

"Don't you ever get tired of travelling? Doesn't your family miss you? Surely, it would be much easier for you to simply share the burden with a few senior animals in your Sanctuary?" reasoned Twit, snidely.

"Such are the heavy burdens of leadership, my dear Twit. Of course, I get terribly weary and yes, my family does miss me. But, as the leader of this Forest's most important development Sanctuary, I cannot but take my responsibilities with the utmost seriousness. I simply have to undertake all this personally, as it would just not do to delegate such crucial activities to anyone. It's so easy to sit in the office and create drawings, or supervise actual work. But the travel that falls so heavily on my shoulders can be handled only by the most senior person," explained Donkey, smoothly.

"I understand. It's just that I was picking up some vague murmurs from some Forest Auditors about most of it being wasteful and unnecessary," pressed Twit, being a tenacious media bird.

"Huh! What do those idiots know about top level management requirements and Sanctuary imperatives! They are just jealous that I get to travel to such exotic Forests frequently, but they forget what a huge burden it is for me personally. Just forget them, Twit," said Donkey, with annoyance.

"Anyway, I was just wondering if I could get an exclusive from you on the various projects in your Sanctuary. It would, sort of, give me an edge over the rest of the media birds, you know."

This was just the sort of vague query Donkey loved, and he brightened, "Now, that's a far more sensible topic to discuss, my dear! As you know, Twit, ours is the most important development Sanctuary in this Forest, and we have over twenty projects in various stages of construction. These will all immensely improve the lives of all animals in our Forest, and make this the most envied Forest in the world. As you know, under the inspired leadership of King Lion, we are taking an aggressively dynamic approach to holistic development of the macro socio-economic sphere, and I untiringly, personally, ensure nothing holds up work on any of our projects, for any reason.

No wonder, "Sanctuary World" recently awarded me the title of "Most Decisive Sanctuary CEA" in the whole Forest." Twit smiled inwardly, knowing that was tied to a substantial financial 'contribution' made to the magazine.

"Wow! That is so very impressive," pretty little Twit batted her eyelashes at him, "I have no doubt King Lion will be immensely pleased with your work. Could you, though, give me some specifics about the actual progress of your developments?"

"I am afraid that is confidential, and only my Board can release such information", smoothly evaded Donkey, with a kindly smile.

"Ah, I quite understand. Never mind. Could you tell me if any of your projects is actually complete?"

"That, too, is confidential information. Sorry."

"Really? Even completed projects are confidential?" stuttered Twit, in disbelief.

"Well...strictly between you and I, Twit, its Minister Ostrich who likes to hog the limelight by making those announcements, rather than let me, the animal that actually did the work, do so. That's the only reason I have to hold back," deflected Donkey.

"But, CEA Donkey, you were the one who presided over all the launches of such completed projects in the past, and gave Minister Ostrich a bit of a secondary role, if you recall," said Twit, not to be put off by Donkey's suave fabrications.

"Ah, yes, of course. But that is the past, you are referring to. Your question relates to the future. And that is what the Minister insists on keeping to himself," Donkey was not to be outdone.

"OK...if you say so. But when can our animal-listeners in the Forest expect to actually see these improvements in their lives?" queried Twit, with more than a modicum of skepticism in her dulcet tones.

"Sorry, Twit, I would have loved to stop and chat, but, as usual, you find me rushing from one crucial meeting to another. With sole responsibility for such a major Sanctuary, and so many very important projects in hand, you can understand how short of time I am. Hundreds of animals are awaiting major decisions from me right now," gushed Donkey, as he quickly rushed off before the media bird could ask any more awkward questions. Twit was becoming unhealthily fixated on silly things like facts and figures. Donkey made a mental note to instruct his Chief Media Brayer to have a quiet word with Twit's Editor about replacing her with a more friendly media bird...or face the prospect of his Sanctuary's huge advertising monies being diverted to rival media channels. Such 'friendly persuasion' never failed to work in this Forest, and it would rid him of even Twit's mildly uncomfortable probing.

However, Twit's picking up vibrations from Forest Audit about his hugely unnecessary travels was cause for disquiet. Of course, no one at his Sanctuary ever dared question his actions. He had expected a measure of discretion even from Forest Audit, in view of his cozy relationship with Minister Ostrich. Clearly, unhappiness there was leaking out, and he needed to find a way to fix it quickly before the dam broke. He continued on his way, deep in thought.

Soon, he ambled into the Forest Clearing Den, with a carefully-cultivated look of being hassled and harassed. "Ah, there you are, Donkey," said Owl levelly, "Just 45 minutes late, this time."

Donkey looked at him in puzzlement. He never could understand Owl's fetish for punctuality. How did it matter, anyway? Life was too short to watch the clock and be over-zealous about efficiency. "Yes, well ... anyway. So, what do you have for me today? As you know, I am very short of time, and will have to rush off very soon to an important meeting with some of our Director Asses."

"Oh, good. In that case, perhaps you could take my project up with them and finally get me their green signal. As you know, my team has been waiting patiently for over six months to begin work. I have repeatedly shown you how this beach bird-bath project would attract hordes of migratory birds, and how that would directly benefit every animal living in our Forest. Surely, that is what our Sanctuary was set up for? What is causing the delay, then? We have worked up very detailed plans, we know exactly how to execute the project, we have located all the resources we need – in short, we do not need anything from you except a simple decision to go ahead!" exclaimed Owl.

Decision! There was the dreaded D word again. And trust Owl to be the one pushing him most aggressively for it. He knew Owl's project was an excellent one and all the Certified Pricing Animals had proved it would immensely benefit the denizens of the Forest. He knew all that, and agreed with all Owl said. The only hitch was that it involved sticking his precious neck out and taking a ... decision! And yet, Owl was a friend...of sorts...whom he respected. For a while, Donkey stared blankly, in desperate confusion (a fairly frequent condition with him, of course). Then, he had it!

"Owl, my friend, as you know, I support your proposal enthusiastically. Unfortunately, I do not have the authority to take a decision on this, and it is up to the Board of Director Asses, who are the ones delaying a decision all these months. I shall go and speak very sternly to them now, and see if we can't push things along finally."

"But, Donkey, this is exactly what you have told me at the last ten meetings we have had! Do they even know what my project is all about, and the benefits that would flow from it to all the animals? After all, you have never allowed me to meet with them myself, let alone present my plans to them," interjected Owl wearily.

"Ahem...yes. Being your friend, I always try very hard to protect you from the irritations of having to deal with the Asses. Believe me, it is no fun. That is why I take the entire heavy burden on my shoulders alone. Of course, I have told them, broadly, very broadly, about your project. They don't really have the time to go into details. The problem is, there are so many issues to deal with, at each Board meeting, that they have just not got around to a decision on your project yet," replied Donkey defensively.

"So busy that they could not arrive at a simple decision after more than six months?" asked Owl, raising a very irritated eyebrow.

Knowing he would not receive a satisfactory answer, Owl went on, "Anyway, what about our own internal clearances for the proposal to go forward to Minister Ostrich? That wretched Skunk has been prevaricating endlessly and raising every nonsensical query he can think of. We can all see through his pathetic delaying tactics. How long are you going to turn a blind eye to such shenanigans?"

"You know how it is, Owl. Anyway, forget all that. I promise I shall be really aggressive with them at the very next meeting, and get you a decision," promised Donkey with practiced smoothness.

"Look, Donkey, being a friend, I have been immensely patient all this time. Now I am beginning to get truly frustrated. Everyone knows this is a great project and we have addressed every single genuine concern that has ever been voiced about it. There should be absolutely no reason to hold it up now. Of course, other than Skunk's stupid antics and perhaps Jackal's politicking. I know he is extremely unhappy about our Sanctuary's biggest single project not being in his hands. For heaven's sake, Donkey, take a stand finally!" the exasperated Owl thundered.

"My dear friend, you are being unfair to me. I back your project fully and enthusiastically, I assure you. Doesn't putting you in charge of our most prestigious project show how much faith I have in you, Owl? And, believe me, Skunk and Jackal are also your friends and support you fully. You probably don't realize it because they praise you so highly behind your back. Anyway, this time, I promise I am really going to kick some Ass – forgive the pun", brayed Donkey loudly, before 'rushing off' to yet another mysterious 'meeting', somewhere in the depths of the Forest.

Owl sighed. He knew it was all a web of fantasy, woven desperately by Donkey, to avoid taking a decision. After all, he himself had served on many

Boards, in many Sanctuaries, and knew perfectly well that it was up to Donkey to take such decisions, and not the Asses on the Board. Since, most unusually at corporate Sanctuaries, every bit of authority in this Sanctuary rested solely in the hoof of Donkey, and no other animal had any decision-making authority, he knew nothing could happen without Donkey's approval. Skunk was just an irritating flunky, even if he did tend to get under Owl's skin with his sliminess. Jackal was another matter altogether. He had a very bad feeling about him and had even warned Donkey on some of the rare occasions when they had a relaxed chat, as friends. Owl was certain Jackal was scheming to undermine Donkey and make a grab for his perch. Only time would tell, he thought resignedly.

Sighing loudly, he wondered, for the hundredth time, whether he should consider leaving this Sanctuary and moving elsewhere ... somewhere he would be allowed to actually do what he did best – create facilities that improved the lives of the animals around. Clearly, joining his friend Donkey's Sanctuary had been a mistake. He had simply allowed Donkey's charm and suave assurances to lull his doubts. In this Sanctuary, he had no access to the Board of Director Asses, or to Minister Ostrich, and so there was no way he could push the project forward. Even internally, within their Sanctuary, Jackal was steadily strengthening his own position and pushing Owl to a corner, as a non-native of their Forest. Utterly two faced, he had become adept at pretending to be Donkey's good friend, to his face, and, behind his back, undermining him with their colleague animals and even the Asses, to all of whom he had free access, being a born native of the Forest. Being an expatriated animal was becoming a serious career liability in this Sanctuary, and he realized he had to make his own decision soon. He was unlikely to be able to stand this indolent drifting and intense politicking much longer.

Chapter 2

Donkey & Skunk

Meanwhile, Donkey skipped happily off, greatly relieved to have been able to deflect Owl's latest attack and, once again, having deftly avoided committing himself in any substantive way. While he respected Owl, there was no doubt that he was rapidly becoming a problem. It seems his kettle was coming to a boil, and Donkey wondered uneasily how much damage an explosion from Owl could do to him. Knowing Owl's reputation and track record, as well as the fact that most media birds looked very favorably on him, Donkey's options were somewhat limited. There was no way he could move overtly against Owl - especially as he had actually done wonders with the beach bird bath project since he took it over – but something surely had to be done, if he was to protect his own hide. However, try as hard as he did, he just could not think of a solution that would ensure he continued to smell of roses. Why, oh why, did these animals have to make his life so very difficult, when all he ever tried to do was for their own good! The heavy burdens of leadership stooped his shoulders.

Looking up from nibbling a tempting bit of stinking rubbish lying beside the path, he spotted little Skunk rushing in search of him. No one knew what Skunk's exact role in the Sanctuary was, least of all Donkey himself. Around the same time he had persuaded Owl to join their Sanctuary, Skunk had somehow managed to evade Donkey's faithful Secretarimal and insinuated himself into Donkey's office, with his smooth, oily patter and flattering subservience. Donkey had been so impressed with Skunk's very impressive, and utterly bogus, Resume that he had not bothered to check any of his references or even do a routine background check, as was normal procedure, before taking him on as his assistant, confidante, advisor and, as he admitted smugly only to himself, his personal servant. Skunk, for his part, knew his ‘illustrious’ career was a clever fabrication, and anxiously pandered to Donkey’s every whim and fancy, ensuring Donkey become completely dependent on him. Early on, he had understood Donkey's character, and worked hard to win himself a permanent niche in his affections by serving as Donkey’s faithful Greek chorus. Since self-respect had never been one of Skunk’s failings, this role fitted him like a glove. It had, for him, the highly desirable result of ensuring Donkey never decided to look too closely into his near non-existent professional expertise. Donkey, for his part, considered Skunk a soul brother. Here was an animal with such obvious intellectual brilliance and depth of expertise and one who was, above all – purely coincidentally - always in agreement with Donkey’s own views! He gave himself a mental pat for having recognized Skunk's immense talent and recruited him. CEAs at other Sanctuaries, who laughed at him behind his back were, he knew, simply resentful at not having got hold of him themselves.

Donkey smiled indulgently as he watched Skunk hurry up to him. “Hail, o great Donkey,” greeted Skunk, bowing low as always. His distinctive cologne infused the air all around. Donkey was probably the only animal at the Sanctuary whose olfactory system was immune to him.

“Skunk, how many times have I asked you not to greet me like that? I am not some emperor – just the greatest CEA in the Forest”, Donkey smiled kindly.

“But you are greater than an emperor to me, o great Donkey. I am always in awe of the sheer power of your mind, and my only wish in life is to humbly learn at your feet,” said Skunk, with lowered eyes – lowered primarily to conceal the amusement sparkling in them.

“Yes, yes, of course. I understand. Anyway, why were you looking for me?”

“In my humble little way, I have again been able to save you having to make a decision, Donkey sir. Jackal was making a nuisance of himself again, asking for all sorts of sanctions, and being rudely aggressive about everything. And Peacock was, as usual, giving himself airs about the hundreds of animal hotels he has ‘personally’ built and wanting authorization to travel to half a dozen distant Forests for some vague workshop. If he has such vast experience, why does he need to attend more workshops anyway?" huffed Skunk.

Donkey smiled, as this was an almost daily bit of entertainment that he secretly enjoyed watching. While his underlings squabbled, he could posture as the benign overload who eventually brought peace to everyone with his wise and kind-hearted decisions! Poor Skunk took most of the beatings at such encounters, as he was also an expatriated animal, and Jackal made the most of his vulnerabilities. However, both Jackal and Peacock knew not to push him too far, for fear of annoying Donkey.

"So, what did you do?" queried Donkey, mildly.

"I fought them valiantly with my great mind – made so sharp by your wisdom - and managed to put a stop to both, by agreeing enthusiastically and promising to include them in the agenda for the next Board of Director Asses meeting. Of course, I shall do no such thing, and later we can simply blame the Asses for refusing their requests. That way, you will not have to make any commitments, and, at the same time, remain the most popular CEA this Sanctuary has ever had," concluded Skunk triumphantly.

"You are a wonder, Skunk," said Donkey with real enthusiasm, "What would I have done without you! So what else has been happening at the Sanctuary, while I have been away at all these vital meetings around the Forest?"

"Quite a lot! As usual, I have been keeping my ears close to the ground, on your behalf. First of all, it seems that Jackal is having a very covert affair with Peacock's Secretarimal. No one seems to have guessed yet, except me! What do you think of that?"

"Ahh..." said Donkey, with amusement. Skunk was disappointed at his response to this juicy bit of gossip, but soldiered on.

"The Forest Audit rats have been nosing around the new animal hotel projects, and there seems to be something smelly there, in Peacock's design domain. I am not sure exactly what it is that they are trying to cover up from the rats, but I am sure I will find out soon."

"That sounds a bit worrying. Please burrow into that as quickly as you can. As you know, the Forest Audit rats are already asking uncomfortable questions about my travels. Now, if they find something in Peacock's domain, it could spell big trouble," said Donkey, with a frown.

"Unfortunately, that is not all. You remember the joint venture we have with Engineer Apep, of the Heaped Stones Forest? His are, by far, our biggest projects, watched closely by Minister Ostrich and even by King Lion himself. Not only are they creating a bigger and bigger mess there, but Apep has, yet again, dismissed his Chief Executive Animal!" informed Skunk.

"What! Yet again? He must have run through about six CEAs in the last six years! This is terrible, and will certainly create a stink 'on high'. What was that wretched Apep thinking? Can't he get along with anyone!" burst out Donkey, his cheerful day now decisively ruined.

"I knew the situation there would create trouble for you, and so I have been very busy digging into it, to find a way to deflect all blame from you to Apep."

"How would that even be possible? We do own 30% of their Sanctuary, and I was supposed to keep a close eye on their activities, on behalf of our Forest. Of course, I did not do anything at all, as I trusted Apep completely. After all, the animal that takes me for such wonderful holidays – oops, workshops, I mean – to the Heaped Stones Forest, and even to the Snowy Mountains Forest, clearly can be trusted completely. I left it entirely in his hands. Now, how will I explain this away?" fretted Donkey.

"I am sure we will be able to think up a convincing story. Don't worry, Donkey sir, just leave it in my hands. I know their projects are a total mess and that all the animals in that Sanctuary are totally demoralized and unhappy. Apep is a megalomaniac who is convinced he is god's gift to the animal kingdom.

Unfortunately, he does not have a clue about how to actually build communities. The one he talks so much about, in the Heaped Stones Forest, is, as you know, a messy, low-quality execution. He tried to do the same here, but grossly over-reached. Now, it is up to us to clean up his mess. But don't worry, Donkey sir, I shall surely find a way to place the blame squarely on Apep, where is really belongs, and ensure you are seen as just a victim of your goodness," soothed Skunk, rising magnificently to his role.

"You are really my best asset, Skunk. Thank you."

Skunk smiled modestly, and went on, "I was rushing over from those meetings, to try and save you having to deal with that wretched Owl all by yourself. You know what he is like – always insisting on decisions and timelines and feasibilities and heavens knows what else. We know his is an excellent project which would benefit all animals. But he just does not seem to understand corporate politics at all. The only way for a CEA to have a happy, peaceful and admired tenure in office is to avoid decisions, avoid risks, even if illusory, avoid difficult questions, and, instead, increase his media profile with happy promises of a rosy dawn in the suitably misty future. After all, to be a really successful CEA, one has to be clever, not necessarily deliver."

Skunk continued, "By the way, Donkey sir, did you hear that Owl has been speaking against you? Just yesterday, one of our Certified Pricing Animals mentioned to me, in confidence, that Owl suggested to him that you are power mad and hence keep all authority with yourself. The cheek!"

"Really? Did he actually say that? Who was the CPA who told you this?" asked Donkey, mildly.

"Now, now, Donkey sir, you know I have to keep my sources confidential, if I am to continue to ferret information out for you. Just trust me. I know he has even suggested that the Board of Director Asses should remove you altogether! Many animals say they don't understand what you see in him," smirked Skunk.

"Hmm..." murmured Donkey, with mild disbelief, "He has a tremendous reputation in this Forest for integrity, delivering results and turning disasters to successes. I am a bit skeptical about these statements about him, but do keep your ears open. Perhaps there is a side to Owl that I am not aware of."

Despite the worrisome news about Apep and the Forest Audit, most of the rest of the gossip was music to Donkey's long ears and he again congratulated himself on acquiring Skunk as his enchanted mirror. They wandered contentedly on through the Forest, sharing bits of idle gossip and Skunk fulminating against Owl and his schemes. After a while, Donkey tuned out and mentally floated off on a haze of self adulation. Perhaps, it might not be such a bad day after all, he mused.

Chapter 3

Donkey & Jackal

Donkey was still in his happy daze, late next morning, when he eventually wandered lazily into his beautiful corner office at the Sanctuary. He had ensured he had, by far, the biggest office in the Sanctuary, with lovely picture windows providing a panoramic view over that neck of the Forest. He had ensured there was no stinting of resources when it came to decorating his office. It had been quite easy to get the compliant CPAs to cover his budgetary excesses by cutting back sharply on the rest of the offices at the Sanctuary. They, like him, understood that the CEA was the most important animal in their lives and his happiness equaled their happiness.

Waiting impatiently for him, outside his office, was his childhood friend and general buddy, Jackal. Despite knowing Jackal was professionally quite incompetent, which he had proven at several other Sanctuaries, Donkey had taken him on, and promoted him to Chief of Animal Buildings. And now, he was trying to push the Board Asses to elevate him even further, to Chief Operating Animal, or COA. After all, what are friends for, Donkey had reasoned, benignly? Jackal was his closest friend and confidant of many, many years. And, as Donkey calculated, surprisingly shrewdly, Jackal would be the ideal buffer between him and not just dreaded decision-making, but also work of any sort. As COA, Jackal would be left with the heavy lifting, while he, Donkey, would be entirely free to concentrate on his media image and on wandering happily around distant, exotic Forests, with no clear objective or agenda. His passion for miles was even greater than that of Peacock and Jackal combined. For over two years, Donkey had been pushing the Asses to agree to this happy resolution, but they were being unreasonably difficult. They lacked, completely, Donkey's own clear-sighted vision and deep understanding of animal nature. But if Donkey was anything, he was stubborn and he was determined to achieve this for his dear friend and ally. He would gnaw at the Asses' behinds till they were so sore they would finally give in to Donkey's wishes. Dear old Jackal, he reflected, my trusted and faithful buddy!

Of course, Jackal had his own ideas. Loyalty did not exist in his vocabulary, and his covert but unerring focus was on replacing Donkey as CEA. Realizing that Donkey's competence was even less than his own, he worked hard at constantly reminding Donkey of their childhood friendship, in myriad subtle ways every day, and on thinking up ingenious schemes to cover up both his and Donkey's inadequacies. Admittedly, he ensured a little of Donkey's inadequacies still showed through – after all, it would not do to have the Asses completely blinded by Donkey's supposed achievements. He had to keep very carefully showing up the chinks in the unwary Donkey's armor, bit by bit, so that he would eventually stand totally exposed, and the Asses would have no option but to turn to Jackal as their savior, appointing him CEA instead. It was an intricate game-plan, but Jackal was far more adept at political manipulation than he would ever be at building things. It was yet another reason for him to palm off the real responsibilities of engineering to someone else, preferably some genuinely experienced but subservient animal, as quickly as possible, before any misadventure exposed his own frailties. Of course, he would painstakingly nurture the appearance of having to shoulder ever greater responsibilities, and constantly having to 'advise' the engineer animals, out of the bottomless wells of his 'immense' construction experience. Jackal was a deep and genuinely devious animal, who would never hesitate to consume anything in his path, even an old friend who trusted him implicitly.

Switching on his usual oily smile, he greeted Donkey, "How are you this morning, my dear old friend? I missed seeing you the whole day yesterday, thanks to the interference of that idiot Skunk. I really don't know what you see in him. If he did not have your protection, I would have been at the head of the queue to eat him up! Believe me! Anyway, listen, I have a great idea to discuss with you."

"Come into my office, Jackal. And leave poor Skunk alone. You know he is a devoted servant of mine. He has such brilliant ideas, which, amazingly, always seem to mirror my own! A really great guy!" enthused Donkey innocently. Then he added, with a slight, sly smirk, "Why, just yesterday, he saved me having to take a bunch of decisions on travel."

"Whatever," grated Jackal, struggling to hide his annoyance, "Anyway, I have an idea that could help both you and I. You know how you have frequently complained about Owl, who keeps bothering you for action all the time. Fortunately, his big beach bird-bath project is stalled – and, between you and I, we can probably quietly kill it off altogether – leaving him with resources he does not need. At the same time, you know I have a huge bunch of projects in my division, for which I desperately need more engineer animals and flying carpets to transport both animals and materiel."

"Come now, Jackal, you have only a couple of small animal hotels to build, and not much is happening on them, anyway," reasoned Donkey. But, not wanting to hurt his friend's feelings, he hastened to add, "Not that I have ever complained about that. As you know, I am a great believer in the old adage that slow and steady wins the race. The slower the steadier, if you ask me."

"That situation is due entirely to my shortage of resources. I could do so much more, for you to show off to the Board Asses, if only I had more resources. Now, here's my plan – and it's a real beauty, even if I say so myself. You could get Owl out of your hair, and help me deliver on my projects at the same time, if you just transfer all Owl's engineer animals and flying carpets to me, leaving him to wither on the vine, without any obvious subversion by you."

"Hmm...Owl certainly is becoming a real pain in my neck, always pushing for decisions and deadlines. Though he is a friend...of sorts...I now wish I had never brought him onboard. He just does not understand Sanctuary politics. After all, as *you* understand so well, at our level of seniority, appearances are so much more crucial than actual actions. Now, as far as your plan goes, he might just conceivably lend you some of his engineer animals, but I know he will not part with Bear, his chief assistant, or his flying carpets," responded Donkey, pensively, "We need to be careful not to underestimate him."

"Let *me* try, Donkey. Even if he keeps just Bear and one flying carpet, he will, in effect, be crippled and can safely be left to rot unnoticed in a remote corner of our Sanctuary. That will take care of pesky Owl, and I can make real progress on our other projects. Which will, of course, give you plenty to show off to the media birds? Just think of that!" said Jackal, with sly innocence.

"Well, I don't know. I can see how it would help me with the media birds, but its Owl after all...oh, okay, you try. But don't tell him it was my idea, and don't blame me if you fail," gave in Donkey, rather nervously. He knew Jackal was hugely under-estimating Owl, but was happy to have it off his own bony shoulders. However, as Jackal slunk away, Donkey's mind turned pensively to the latest snide rumor Skunk had dropped into his overtaxed little brain. It seemed some people believed Jackal was taking brown envelopes from vendor animals. Being an honest animal himself, he could not quite bring himself to believe this of Jackal, especially as he had been his closest friend since their early childhood. At the same time, it was something that he could not completely ignore, however unpleasant it was for him personally. Sometimes, he sighed, I wish I had a sandbox, like Minister Ostrich, into which I could bury my head and make the world go away. He was worrying needlessly, he was certain; his dear friend could never ever let him down in any way.

Meanwhile, as he loped deeper into the shadowy undergrowth he loved above all other places, Jackal gloated, "That is all the approval I need, to swallow Owl and his division entirely, like old Boa Constrictor."

He headed directly for Owl's nest, deep inside the Forest, twitching his nose in delightful anticipation. His day had finally dawned. He was smugly certain he had hit on the perfect ploy to oust Owl and expand his own empire, within their Sanctuary.

Jackal found Owl perched peacefully on his branch, lost in thought, as usual, and greeted him ingratiatingly, hoping to put him off his guard, "Oh hi, Owl, my dear friend. How are you this fine day?"

Owl looked coolly at Jackal and responded shortly, "As well as can be expected, under the circumstances."

"My dear Owl, I know how busy you are and I hate to disturb you without an appointment. However, I come bearing a message for you from our dear CEA. He believes there is likely to a long delay in getting approvals for your project and so has instructed you to hand over all your engineer animals and flying carpets to my division. As you know, personally, I am a huge enthusiast for your project, and am always willing to extend any support that you might need, but we both know it's hardly likely that Minister Ostrich will sanction a high-profile investment like bird-baths on the beach! So, the CEA feels your resources would be better utilized on my many ongoing animal hotels. Of course, *I* had nothing to do with the idea at all, and only reluctantly accepted the order because it came directly from the CEA himself. After all, *I* would never try to take anything from *you*, my dear friend. It's all his doing. But, you know, when the CEA orders, we lesser animals simply have to obey."

"Indeed!" mused Owl, "He was with me just yesterday, and it's strange that he did not mention any of this then."

"Perhaps it just slipped his mind at the time. You know how overloaded with work he is. Anyway, I have just come from him, with these orders."

"I see. I have no objection to your having Engineer Snake. I know you were his mentor because he is from your neck of the woods. However, I find him arrogant, disloyal and incompetent. You are most welcome to him. I can give you Engineer Hog on loan, but only till my own project comes to life, as I know it definitely will, sooner or later. Neither Donkey nor Ostrich will be able to sit on a decision on such an obviously beneficial project for much longer, despite what you may think. So, you can have him on loan strictly for a limited period. And I can let you have one of my two flying carpets. That's it, CEA's orders or not."

"But the CEA said I could have *all* your resources," whined Jackal, "You cannot flout the CEA's orders. I must have them, or else."

"Or else, what?" asked Owl, with cold menace, quietly clicking his razor-sharp beak.

Jackal took a hasty step back, realizing he had over-stepped the mark. After all, the CEA had issued no such orders and only he could do so, not Jackal. Moreover, if Owl recounted this conversation to Donkey, it would be, well, embarrassing, to say the least. Placatingly, he simpered, "Nothing, nothing. I just meant to say or else my animal hotels will be badly delayed."

"If you cannot manage your few little jobs with the many resources you have, that is your problem, not mine," said Owl, bluntly.

"Of course, of course, you are quite right. By the way, you have not mentioned giving me Engineer Bear ..." Jackal's voice choked in terror at the look of fury in Owl's eyes. Hastily, he made his escape back into the undergrowth of the Forest. Having run far enough to feel safe again, Jackal paused for breath and pondered. He had made major gains, but was still far from swallowing Owl's entire group. He had thought Owl would be the softest target in the Sanctuary, the ideal one to start his conquests with. Clearly he had underestimated him. But it's not over yet, Jackal grimly vowed, not by a long chalk. By the time I am done with him, there will not a single grey feather left. As soon as I am CEA, he thought. Jackal had always suffered from a major Genghis Khan complex.

Chapter 4

Jackal, Peacock & Ant

Jackal headed towards his area of the Sanctuary, quietly fuming and nursing his wounded ego. As he turned into a small clearing, he came upon his close friend and co-conspirator, Peacock. As he often did, Peacock was busy admiring his beautiful plumage and prancing happily around, oblivious to the world. Jackal smiled indulgently. It was all right for Peacock to indulge his harmless little foibles – just so long as he continued to arrange for Jackal's frequent luxurious jaunts to exotic Forests around the world, and generally supported him in his quest for the holy grail of CEA. How Peacock managed to get Donkey to approve these many jaunts, which, he had to admit to himself, had not the slightest justification or need, he never could figure out. It would be a useful trick to master, he mused.

Suddenly, catching sight of him, Peacock brightened, "Hi there, Jackal. What do you think of these new feathers I have grown in my fan? They are utterly awesome, aren't they?"

"Yes, yes, very nice, Peacock," said Jackal impatiently.

"Oh, by the way, the Stargazers Group are so stunned with the breadth of my animal hotel building experience around the world, they think I am one of the greatest living designers in the world. I know you agree. And, get this! They want to sponsor you and I for an all-expenses paid jaunt to their newest hotel, Las Vorest, all the way across the seven seas, in the Sunset Lands! What a fabulous holiday – oops, I mean workshop – that will be for us," giggled Peacock, "And all we have to do is give them the management contract for the animal hotels we are building at the moment. Of course, we know they are the most expensive bidder of all, but we will have to somehow 'massage' our systems to get them in. After all, we can hardly be expected to give up such a fabulous trip over a silly thing like a competitive bid."

"That is great news, Peacock. Thanks for including me, as always. Of course, we will find some loophole in our systems to get Stargazers in. We have done it before. However, you must remind them about the brown envelopes we require as well."

"Already done, and they are perfectly comfortable with it. They do business all over the world and are quite used to the brown envelope system. In fact, they have already included our 10% in their bid. So, start packing, my friend!" responded Peacock.

"What about Donkey's approval? You know we cannot go without the CEA's hoof mark. And he just might sniff some conflict of interest, you know, especially with that wretched Skunk grinding his own axe at our expense," worried Jackal.

"Ah ha, I have already got it!" gloated Peacock, "As usual, I managed to sneak past Skunk when he was not looking and then it was just a piece of grain to convince him about the vital importance of this workshop, especially as I have promised him a trip as well, in due course. As for conflict of interest, do you really think he understands the meaning of the words?" laughed Peacock, "Of course, when he found out, Skunk tried to be his usual obnoxious, obstructionist self, but I had already grabbed Donkey's hoof mark, so there was nothing he could do about it!"

"You are quite a magician, my dear Peacock, the way you always manage to get Donkey's hoof mark on anything we need!" Jackal congratulated his friend, "While we are there, we should try and visit as many animal casinos as we can. I assume, as usual, Stargazers will provide us with the cash to do justice to the casinos?"

"That's for sure. And they have promised us other delights as well. I can't wait to get there!"

Well pleased, Jackal trotted off down the path, to his own lair, where he had a meeting with the Head Ant of the Worker Ants Construction Co., who were hoping to be awarded the job of building the only, tiny, animal dwelling project that his division actually had on hand (which had to somehow masquerade as the many important projects he constantly claimed, to anyone who would listen).

Head Ant was waiting patiently for him in the lair. He was well aware that Jackal had no compunctions about keeping vendors waiting, as a power play. Jackal seated himself importantly, and spent several minutes unnecessarily fiddling around with various items on his work space. It was vital to impress his importance on all these contractors, so as to achieve the only major objective he had in all such negotiations - the size of his brown envelope.

"I am afraid I don't have much time, as I am extremely busy with all our complicated building projects," he began curtly, "Please tell me quickly what it is you want."

"Jackal, sir, you are our most respected client and we only seek to enhance your glory in any way we can. At the moment, we are very keen to serve you by taking on the contract to build your animal dwellings. We know we will lose in executing this contract, but, for you, we are willing to suffer anything," Ant enthused with practiced ease, knowing well that contracts from this particular Sanctuary were always unbelievably well padded for contractors.

"That's all very well. But I notice you have under-specified the main beams of the complex. That is quite unacceptable, you know."

"I hardly need explain to an expert like you that our under-specified beams will hold up for long enough. After all, every bit of resource we save there goes into your brown envelope. So, as you can see, my dear Jackal sir, that as well as the other under-specifications that I would beg you to ignore, are all there for your benefit. As I said earlier, we live to serve you, sir," explained Head Ant confidently.

"Excellent, excellent. In that case, there is just one key issue to discuss, and then we can put our paw prints on it. The issue of my brown envelope, of course. How much is in it for me?" asked Jackal without preamble.

"But naturally. We have already covered you for 5%, sir," responded Ant with a big smile.

"Are you joking, Ant? 5%? What do you think I am? Some stray animal wandered in off the forest pavement? How dare you!" thundered Jackal, with well-staged anger.

"Sir, sir, please don't be annoyed. Of course, we can increase it to the full 10% for you. After all, you are Jackal, the greatest building engineer animal in our Forest, and the inspiration of all worker ants. It will go into your usual numbered account in the Snowy Mountains Forest, I assume, sir?"

"Yes, of course. And, as usual, you will absolutely ensure that not even a whisper of our arrangement reaches the ears of Donkey. He has strange, antediluvian ideas about these simple realities of life."

"What arrangement?" Head Ant smiled innocently, to Jackal's delight.

"And, of course, you will also throw in a bone for my friend Peacock, won't you? We do need him playing on our team," asked Jackal.

"Oh, we have already taken care of Peacock. As you know, our arrangements with him are directly in the Snowy Mountains Forest," responded Head Ant.

"Very well then, we are in agreement on all matters. Where is the contract for my paw print?" asked Jackal.

This was quickly produced and a very satisfied Ant scurried away with the valuable paw print. He was going to become even richer, thanks to the corrupt and unethical Jackal. He grinned happily. Such animals were always the easiest to handle. It was always a matter of their personal price and that, being well known, was always added into the contract price. Everyone was happy – except, perhaps, the consumer. But then, who cared about the consumer anyway! Such was the beauty of Government contracts in this Forest.

Jackal, too, was happy. He leaned back, put his paws on the rock, and lit up the expensive cigar another supplier animal had been honored to present him with. Weighing the gains and losses of his day, so far, he was well satisfied with the way things were going. It was a fine day!

Chapter 5

Ostrich & Possum

Minister Ostrich was very annoyed. The representatives of the foreign Sanctuary had changed everything in the Agreement he had personally drafted and sent them almost two months ago. The cheek! As soon as King Lion had instructed him to hand over Owl's beloved beach bird-bath project to the foreigners, he had wasted no time in doing as he had been told. Of course, he had conveniently 'forgotten' to mention this fact to Donkey or Owl himself. The handover was a shame, really, he mused, as Owl's project would have benefited all the animals in the Forest hugely, and if he had been able to pick up the courage to explain this to King Lion, of course he would never have given the project away to foreigners. However, like any good politician, Ostrich, was focused on his own self-interest, and not some vague national interest. As a trusted, effective Minister, he knew when to shove his head decisively into his sandbox. And, of course, he had done so, and sent off what he still believed to be an excellent Agreement to the foreigners. And now they had returned it to him, awash in red ink! That was the problem with foreigners, wasn't it? They just did not understand politics. All they really needed to do was quickly hoof-mark the document, take over the place, and then do whatever they wished – or, more likely, do nothing at all. No one would be any the wiser, least of all King Lion. His friendship with the king of the foreign Forest would be sealed with the mutual defence treaty against attacks by the huge pack of Rabid Hyenas from across the water. And King Lion would be acutely aware that he, Minister Ostrich, had been instrumental in achieving it. A clear win-win for all, as he saw it. And now, the wretched foreigners were complicating matters by insisting on changes and causing delays; inserting deadlines, of all things! If Donkey or, heaven forbid, Owl, heard of the deal before it was hoof-marked and sealed, there would be hell to pay, he knew. Owl's great track-record was known to many Ministers, who all respected him, while Donkey was very well networked, thanks to his unflagging, self-focused public relations efforts. They could cause serious political discomfort to Minister Ostrich. And the wretched Owl was disgustingly unimpressed with his lofty Ministerial stature and status.

He knew the key was to remain, officially, ignorant of Owl's plans and the benefits they would bring to all the animals. To this end, thus far, he had striven mightily to evaded all efforts by Donkey and Owl to meet with him and had not let the project even appear on any meeting agenda. That way, when the dark deed was done, he could play the innocent and claim he was never informed of Owl's plans till it was too late. And, anyway, he had done it, oh so reluctantly, against his own wishes, because of orders from "on high". Who could then blame poor innocent Ostrich? It was, however, now becoming a bit difficult to think up new excuses for delay, and hence speed was of the essence. If only these wretched foreigners would understand that.

He sighed, and rang for his henchanimal, Possum, to try and work out a way to speed things up with the foreigners. After all, unlike him, they thought highly of Possum, for some strange reason.

"You summoned me, Your Excellency?" whispered Possum, breathlessly.

"Yes, yes. Just look at what your friends have done to our lovely Agreement! This is outrageous! How could you let it happen? What am I going to tell King Lion now?" raged Ostrich.

"Your Excellency, the points they make are quite reasonable, as you will see, if you read them," said Possum, holding his ground courageously, "Anyway, are you certain we really want this deal? Did you explain to King Lion the huge benefits our animals would get if we executed Owl's project ourselves?"

"How dare you question me, Possum!" thundered Ostrich, "Do you think I am crazy enough to explain anything to the mighty King Lion? It's his wish and that is good enough for me! Is it not good enough for you?" Ostrich snarled, threateningly.

"Of course it is," Possum hastily back-peddled. It was one thing to take on Minister Ostrich but quite another to even seem to contradict King Lion. Possum was under no illusions as to where that would lead. "What are your wishes now? I shall carry them out immediately."

"I can't be bothered to read what they have written. Just talk to your friends and sort it out so that we can paw print it quickly. I must be able to revert to King Lion with good news before the moon festival."

"I shall take care of it," confirmed Possum, all fight now gone out of him.

"And, of course, you will ensure that not a whisper of this leaks out to Donkey or Owl. If I hear even a rumor that it has, I will definitely have your head. Don't suffer under any illusions, Possum – this is a national priority negotiated by King Lion himself," said Ostrich, angrily.

"I shall take care of everything, sir" said Possum again, humbly, "May I broach another subject while I am here?

"What is it now?" asked Ostrich, somewhat mollified.

"There is an important convention being held in the Sunset Lands next month, which would be very useful for me to attend. May I have your approval to do so?

"Certainly not, Possum. I am aware of the convention, and I intend to attend it myself. There is no need for you to travel as well," returned Ostrich, to Possum's great disappointment, and secret resentment.

He bowed submissively, and wandered disconsolately back to his hole. Unknown to Ostrich, Possum had already hinted at this development to his friend, Owl. Possum was very unhappy with this handover, despite the fact that the foreigners in question were also friends of his. He could clearly see how beneficial this project would have been for their Forest, and, as one of the Director Asses of this Sanctuary, he had fought long and hard to get it approved, before King Lion, losing patience, decided to give it away, in exchange for a mutual defence treaty. Now, there was just no way out and he would have to go through with it. Possum could not help feeling like he was betraying his Forest – and Owl – despite the fact that it was not his decision.

Meanwhile, Minister Ostrich contemplated the short-lived confrontation with his subordinate. That Possum was becoming too big for his paws and something needed to be done. All Ministry animals knew implicitly that unquestioning obedience to their Minister's will was an unshakeable credo. So, what had possessed a veteran like Possum to even mildly challenge him? And this was not the first time he had done so. Had he forgotten that his protector, Ostrich's predecessor, was no longer around? Yes, something would have to be done about Possum, and soon. After mulling it over for a while, Minister Ostrich sighed again, and quickly stuck his head back into the safe, comforting sandbox on his table. Unlike poor Donkey, he did have an effective way of making all unpleasantness just vanish.

Chapter 6

Jackal & Peacock

Jackal was in trouble. A crisis had suddenly blown up out of a clear, blue sky and taken him completely unawares. There was now a serious risk of his nexus with Peacock being exposed to the pitiless light of day – and that just would not do. Someone apparently had dropped a hint in Donkey's ear about their cozy little arrangement at the discreet bank in the Snowy Mountains Forest. Suddenly, for the first time, Donkey had declined to approve their latest junket to the Sunset Lands. Peacock, being an expatriate animal, could, at any time, simply fly away. But he, Jackal, had his roots deep in this Forest and there was simply no way he could allow any hint of scandal to touch him. Once again, he thumped his throbbing forehead against the tree, and wondered who the informer could be. Surely it could not have come from the dreaded Forest Audit team who had been ferreting around the Sanctuary for the last few months? That was just too awful to contemplate. Who then could it be? It was probably Skunk, he decided. It appeared to have all the hallmarks of Skunk. He would get even with him, Jackal vowed angrily, if it was the last thing he did. Donkey would not be able to protect him forever, and Jackal would be waiting in the shadows, to pounce and devour that wretched creature. The Forest would be a far better place without Skunk, he knew.

Suddenly, he brightened. Perhaps he could turn this on Peacock and make him the scapegoat. The only animal Jackal was really loyal to was, of course, himself, and, if it served his purpose, he would not hesitate to sacrifice his fellow conspirator. He racked his devious brain to think up a suitable scheme to deflect all suspicion from himself and on to the unsuspecting Peacock. After all, he was not known as the Machiavelli of the Forest for nothing, he chuckled, grimly.

Fortunately for Jackal, Peacock was a vainglorious animal, completely engrossed in admiring his own, rather suspect, skills and expertise. He was realist enough to understand how hollow they actually were, beneath the public sheen he constantly gave them, and knew that he needed a powerful local protector animal, to cover up for him. He also understood well that only shared, illicit interest could bind them tightly enough to protect him in the longer term. Peacock knew he was getting on in years and that he could not fool any other Sanctuary, anywhere, into having him. So, it was essential to find a protector animal quickly and tie him in, deep and strong.

Fairly early on, after arriving at Donkey's Sanctuary, Peacock had realized his best bet was the slippery and incompetent Jackal – a professional soul-mate, if ever there was one! He had also quickly seen through to Jackal's money-grubbing soul, and taken note of his love of the fast life in some of the exotic Forests of the world, most especially the Sunset Lands and his own Snowy Mountain Forest. Assiduously, Peacock had set about winning him to a partnership to protect their shared professional hollowness, and set up the very discreet account in the Snowy Mountains Forest, topping it all with a lavish coating of junkets to a luscious overseas Forest at least every month, on the excuse of design workshops, discussions with foreign collaborator animals, meetings with specialist animals and just about every excuse his fertile brain could invent. He also delivered a slew of exciting designs (mostly stolen off the Animalnet) for Jackal to present to Donkey as his own ideas. So far, this arrangement had worked out better than his wildest expectations. He knew he had Jackal in his snare, and, for some reason, Jackal appeared to have some sort of a hold over Donkey. It was a highly satisfactory state of affairs for Peacock.

Peacock may have been vainglorious and empty-headed in many ways, but he was a survivor, a shrewd schemer when it came to his own self interest. A sharp pair of eyes and a pair of ears very close to the ground ensured no threat ever crept up on him unawares. Unknown to Jackal, he, too, had heard the ominous rumblings from Donkey's office and his alarm bells had jangled loudly when Donkey turned down the latest of his many requests for travel approval. Storm clouds were, obviously, gathering and Peacock had to look to his precious feathers quickly. He thoroughly understood the opportunistic quality of Jackal's loyalty to him, and knew he had to move rapidly to protect his own back. Jackal had to be made to realize that his future was permanently linked to Peacock's, so that he did not entertain any foolish ideas of heaving this poor expatriate animal over the side, in the storm. He knew the account in the Snowy Mountains Forest ensured this, but perhaps, just perhaps, it was time to think up a Plan B too.

As he pondered the situation bleakly, Jackal suddenly slinked out of the undergrowth behind him. "Ah, Peacock, my dear, dear friend. I have not seen you for hours and missed you sorely. How are you, my dear?" he gushed, as usual.

"Funny you should ask that, my dearest friend in this world!" responded Peacock equally warmly, not fooled for a moment, "I was just thinking of you myself! Have you seen this strange travel rejection from Donkey? What do you make of it?"

"We don't have to worry, Peacock, I happen to know that it has no significance at all. Old Donkey does not care about our travels. I have a feeling it was just Skunk trying to queer the pitch for us, as usual. We really have to come up with a big stick to beat him with. Unfortunately, Donkey protects him and so we have to be very careful. But, for our own sakes, we need to find a way of making him disappear, and the sooner the better."

"Yes," agreed Peacock, "If he were ever to find out about our other arrangements, we could end up in the worst cage in the Forest. He is a cause for concern, especially now, with the Forest Audit snooping around too"

"Neither Donkey nor Skunk knows anything about the Snowy Mountains Forest. Be easy in your mind," Jackal said.

"That's a huge relief. Now I can put that out of my mind and focus on finding a way to deal with Skunk," smoothly lied Peacock.

“Incidentally, I had meant to ask you earlier, does my name actually appear on any of the Snowy Mountains Forest paperwork? After all, we had agreed to use you as our common front,” despite his best efforts, Jackal was unable to entirely hide the quaver in his voice.

“Yes, of course it does. All our arrangements, of every sort, clearly have your name on them. After all, we do not ever want any misunderstandings between dear friends like us, on shares, do we?” beamed Peacock, silently congratulating himself on having accurately guessed Jackal’s true intentions.

“Oh....Yes, yes, of course,” muttered Jackal, unhappily. Was there some way he could pretend that Peacock’s partner was some other Jackal, possibly some foreign Jackal? The pitiless iron jaws of the bear-trap seemed to yawn ever wider at his feet, and he shivered involuntarily.

“Why, my dear friend, is something the matter? I’d swear you look leaner and hungrier than usual,” interjected Peacock slily, with apparent concern.

“No, no, nothing at all. You know what pressures all these projects have placed on me. I was so looking forward to our latest junket. And, of course, a further transmission to the Snowy Mountains Forest would have done no harm at all. Ah, well. I guess we will have to wait a few days and try again.”

“Yes, I believe that is best. And, this time, we will include him in our junket. That will make it difficult for him to turn it down,” chuckled Peacock.

“I do have one piece of good news, though,” continued Jackal after a pause. “I finally managed to persuade Donkey to let me prise Owl’s resources from him. Unfortunately, the stubborn old fool did not hand over everything, but I did manage to get two engineer animals and a flying carpet. It’s the beginning of the end for him, as we planned,” said Jackal with satisfaction.

“Jackal, you are really the most brilliant animal at this Sanctuary!,” exclaimed Peacock, genuinely pleased with the news. “Operation Outflanked Owl” as he labelled it privately, was his brainchild, which he had, as usual, persuaded Jackal was a product of his fertile brain. “So, did he give up Engineer Bear?”

"Nooo.." said Jackal slowly, remembering Owl's furious look, with a shiver, "But he will, in due course. He cannot escape my noose, now that I have begun tightening it."

"Excellent! Excellent! I will get on with absorbing those resources into our division quickly," said Peacock, as Jackal lumbered off into the underbrush again.

"Soooo...," mused Peacock thoughtfully, "I was right. That greasy Jackal is trying to get himself off the hook by throwing me to the Asses. Does he think I am a complete fool, to be taken in by his play acting? Anyway, now he has had a glimpse of the steel in my velvet claw-cover. He should be in no doubt that I hold all the cards. Thank the stars I ensured his name is on the account in the Snowy Mountains Forest. That will keep him safely tied to me. Now, we just need to keep our heads, and let the fuss die down - as it always does. And it surely will. If anything is certain about this Sanctuary, it is the laziness of its animals. But, perhaps, it is time to try and implicate Donkey as well. Just as extra insurance against a rainy day. I wonder what he thinks of brown envelopes."

Chapter 7

Owl & Snake & Bear

While Peacock schemed, Jackal worried, and Donkey sang happily to himself, Owl summoned Engineer Snake to him. When that thoroughly unpopular creature finally slithered up to the foot of his tree, Owl felt the usual shiver of revulsion at his presence. Snake beamed at him, apparently unaware of the universal dislike he inspired, and said, "You sent for me, Boss?"

Overcoming his distaste for the reptile with difficulty, he told him, "Yes. I have been asked by our CEA to transfer you to Engineer Jackal's division. I know he is your protector and mentor, so you can slither off to him immediately– and never return."

Snake put on a well-practiced pained expression. "But, why? I love you dearly and really enjoy working for you. Even though I am the son of a King Cobra, I have never behaved arrogantly, or not done anything you asked of me. After all, I am a true team player and always pull my weight. Moreover, I really love this beach bird-bath project. So, why am I being sent off?" he whined.

Owl swallowed his anger at the obvious hypocrisy of Snake and replied coldly, "You certainly are arrogant and disloyal, and definitely have never been a team player. I don't care whose son you are – thank heavens you are not mine anyway! Do you think I am unaware of all your scheming behind my back with Jackal? So, good riddance to you. Go!"

Snake did not like this turn of events at all. While Jackal was indeed his mentor, a transfer to his division meant he would actually have to do some work, for a change. Because Owl's project site was such a sprawling one, he had been able to successfully hide in one remote area or the other most of the time, and had, largely, had a smooth ride. Jackal's group, on the other hand, worked inside the office and his slacking off would be highly visible and noticed. This would not do at all. He decided to change tack.

“Have you seen this order from the CEA yourself?” he asked.

“No, I have not, but I am willing to accept Jackal’s word for it. Especially since it means I will be rid of you,” responded Owl.

“Have you forgotten whose son I am, Owl? Have you forgotten that I can make life very difficult for you, if you make me unhappy?” hissed Snake angrily. His illustrious heritage was being brazenly ignored!

“You could be the son of the Great Golden Baboon for all I care, you despicable creature,” roared Owl furiously, “There is nothing you can do to me and if you do not slither off this very moment, I shall do quite a bit to you, instead.”

Snake stared at him for a long moment with what, he thought, was a menacing look but one which, in reality, only looked goofy. Then he slithered off quickly into the undergrowth, knowing he was defeated. He would just have to work on Jackal, to make his new berth cushy enough.

“Thank heavens we have seen the last of that wretch,” growled Bear, emerging from the Forest at that moment, “Excuse me, but I happened to overhear your conversation with Snake. May I break out the coconut water?”

Owl laughed. “Yes, it is good riddance to him. He was like a malignant tumor in our team – and I have never felt that way about any subordinate, in all my long years. As we know, Jackal has been scheming for quite some time to swallow up our division, and he now seems to have been able to finally persuade Donkey. That is what he says, anyway. I did not bother to double check with Donkey. Jackal thinks he is stripping me of my key resources. Little does he realize that he has just done me the biggest favor possible, by excising this cancer!”

Bear growled a hearty laugh - he completely shared Owl’s view of Snake.

"Yes, it would have been very difficult to work with him, otherwise. What with his extreme laziness and his constant reminders about his father, King Cobra! What an utterly insufferable reptile."

"Oh, Jackal even tried to make a wild grab for you, Bear. He should really have known better. Just one look from me was enough to put paid to that effort and send him scurrying back to his hole. I swear, those two truly deserve each other!"

"Did he seriously think I would go and work for him?" spluttered Bear incredulously.

"Apparently. He even took one of our flying carpets. Claimed it was all the CEA's orders, to transfer all my engineer animals and flying carpets to him! I know Donkey would never dare issue such an order to me. Anyway, I sent him off with a flea in his ear."

"Enough of those slime-balls," grimaced Bear, "Any news from Donkey?"

"Yet again, he passed the buck on to the Asses, and assured me that he would talk to them very sternly at the next meeting. Exactly what he has said every month for the last many months. I don't know, Bear, I have a bad feeling about this. I doubt our project will ever happen. I keep telling Donkey that he must allow us to present our scheme to Minister Ostrich directly. Once he sees what we have planned, and how massively it would benefit all our animals, I have no doubt he will approve it immediately. Wretched Donkey just does not have the courage to push Ostrich. And I have a shrewd suspicion that our friend, Jackal, is working on the Asses individually, on the side lines, using his "I am like you, an animal from this Forest" trump card, to erode our position further," sighed Owl.

"Is there anything we can do to push things along?" asked Bear in his simple, direct manner.

"I am afraid not. I suspect it is becoming a hot political issue, going all the way up to King Lion. I even heard a hint to that effect from Possum when we last met. Nothing else can explain Minister Ostrich's evasions. In fact, I am so sick of it all, that I am seriously considering flying off to another Sanctuary somewhere. I have just about had it here, with Donkey and Skunk and Jackal and Peacock."

"I know how frustrated you are, Owl, but please don't do that. Think of us, your team. You know Jackal will make mincemeat of us, if you leave. And, anyway, our project has too great a socio-economic significance for this Forest to be allowed to die. Why, even if the foreigners take it over, they will need us to carry it out for them, won't they? After all, they don't know our Forest, and especially our beach" said Bear, with more hope than real confidence.

"Well, let us wait and watch for a while. But I know that things cannot continue this way for much longer. I just cannot bear it – forgive the pun."

Bear stared thoughtfully at him for a while and then shambled off disconsolately, wondering about his own future, amid these political shifting sands that he was so ill equipped to navigate. Owl had personally selected him for his team not only because of his rich experience and teamwork, but also because he was a simple, honest animal who just concentrated on doing his job as well as he possibly could. The one thought that cheered him was that he knew Owl would never abandon him or the other core team members. Owl was too loyal an animal, and his integrity was well known all over the Forest. If Jackal or Donkey pushed too hard, Bear had no doubt that Owl would be picked up very quickly by another Sanctuary and that he would take his team along with him. Comforted by that thought, Bear ambled off to try and create some sort of meaningful work to occupy himself with, despite Donkey having just about brought their beautiful project to a halt.

Watching him go off, Engineer Bear Cub and Secretarimal Deer wondered what was bothering the always cheerful Bear. The three of them formed Owl's core team and worked very well together. Owl was the sort of leader who gave everyone enough autonomy to do their jobs well and ensured their individual achievements are always highlighted to Donkey and the Asses, whenever possible. Looking around the Sanctuary, they knew they were lucky to have a leader who believed in a completely different work ethic. Owl had often told them that he not only wanted them to work efficiently, but, even more, to enjoy their work. On that happy thought, they decided it must just be a passing cloud and turned back to their tasks. After all, they were natives of this Forest and it did not take much for them to return to their usual complacent selves!

Chapter 8

Owl & Panthers

As Owl watched Bear stroll off, his thoughts turned to the last Sanctuary he had worked at. He thought back nostalgically, and less than modestly, to the greatest triumph of his career. He had been CEA of that Sanctuary, tasked with creating the very first recreational warren in the entire Forest. The project had been left in a complete mess by a series of corrupt and incompetent CEAs, who so reminded him of Jackal and Donkey. They had shamelessly taken advantage of the naive Royal Panthers, who owned it, and quietly transferred all the resources of the project to their own accounts in foreign Forests. It was the disgrace of the entire Forest, and no self respecting animal was willing to come anywhere near it, let alone try to fix it. It was rumored that King Lion himself was very displeased about it all. Understandably, then, his friends had been horrified when Owl decided to accept the challenge offered him by Panther, the credulous animal who owned the land but had been the victim of all the confidence trickster animals. Since Panther understood nothing whatsoever about such activities, and much preferred just lying around in the sun, he was more than happy to let Owl have a completely free hand. He had been pleasantly surprised when Owl had actually accepted his offer, and was content to have the project off his hands. The one thing he knew about Owl was his shining reputation for integrity and performance. He, therefore, had had no real expectation that Owl would even consider his offer.

Owl had flown into what was almost a mausoleum. Only a few unhappy animals wandered disconsolately around the ruins, which were full of cobwebs and the smell of defeat. There was no real activity of any sort, and it was obvious that the Forest was merely waiting for it all to collapse. Every bank in the Forest had turned its back on the warren. As soon as they heard of Owl taking over, a long line of angry animals promptly arrived at his doorstep, demanding long overdue payments for services performed. Apparently, a mountain of resources had been spent over the last few years, though there was not the faintest hint of any work on the ground. Since all the furious contractor and supplier animals at his door had never been paid, Owl wondered where all the massive resources had gone. On his very first day, he was made acutely aware that not only would the Forest banks not talk to him, and the contractor animals were out for his blood, but even the would-be users of the warren were furious at not having the facility they had been promised. With a new CEA at the helm, they all finally had a focus for their fury! Owl remembered wondering whether he had been utterly foolhardy in taking up that particular challenge.

It had not taken him long, however, to begin a vigorous clean-up, in his usual direct and aggressive style. He had rapidly convinced the biggest bank in the Forest to support his efforts – suddenly, leading to squeals of agony from the other banks! Using those resources to clear up payments so long overdue to all the animals, including the warren's own animals, he had signaled a new dawn at the project. By then, the media birds had began to express mild curiosity, but, to the Forest at large, there was no visible change on the ground. His own animals had gradually begun to realize that Owl was a man of his word and that he was determined to make things happen, but always in an efficient and ethical manner. Slowly, very slowly, morale had begun to revive, and the first marks of progress had begun to show on the ground.

Within six months, construction on the recreational warren was on in full swing, the clearing in the Forest swarmed with Worker Ants and a flotilla of flying carpets zipped all over the place, busily transporting engineer animals and materials to various parts of the warren. Enthusiasm within the Sanctuary peaked to an unprecedented high, the Forest bank was delighted, the media birds sang happily and Panther was bemused. That first year, Owl's family saw little of him, as he rushed around the Forest and even many foreign Forests, galvanizing every resource he could find into galloping action on his behalf, like there was no tomorrow. He was proud to be the spark that had brought this Sanctuary to life, and he worked happily around the clock.

His family was indulgent and supportive, content to see him so happy. They always had complete faith in his ability to deliver, despite all the odds, and had seen him do so repeatedly in his long career.

Within two years, the recreational warren was complete – the very first in the Forest. Owl perched on a lofty branch and surveyed it all with a satisfied smile - he had actually been able to build it, and that, in record time. There had been times when it had looked doomed to failure, and he had been on the verge of despair, but he had never given up. Now, the fruits of the hard labor of their team of champions, as he thought of them, lay spread out in front of his eyes, in all its glory. The entire Forest was singing the praises of his Sanctuary. He could hardly believe it was already time to open the warren for all the animals to play and live in, and that Minister Ostrich himself was coming to inaugurate it. Mentally, he doffed his hat to the mortally ill Panther, who had allowed him a completely free hand, as the CEA, to make this hugely difficult turnaround possible. That brought him around to consideration of Panther's son, Slug Jr., the lazy, indolent and ignorant inheritor. He hated even the thought of work, much preferring to party with other rich cubs all night long and sleep all day. The only thing Slug actually coveted was Owl's title of CEA. Now that the warren was complete, he knew it had been built so well it could almost run itself, and he could easily assume the CEA's mantle, without having to worry about its responsibilities. Slug was certain he was ready to move into Owl's shoes – indeed that he *must* move into Owl's shoes so as to take all the bows and accolades which were fairly due to Panther's family. After all, Owl had only been a tool, and with the job done, could easily be discarded.

Knowing Panther would never agree to his scheme to ease Owl out, but also knowing that Panther was dying, Slug worked on his Mother, Stork's, maternal sympathies. Unlike Slug, Stork was shrewd enough to realize that openly forcing Owl out would redound to the utter discredit of her family. Moreover, despite herself, she had a lot of respect for Owl's abilities and achievement, having also seen his work at another Sanctuary earlier. So, she quietly set to work behind the scenes to indirectly undermine Owl's position within the Sanctuary, gradually, subtly eroding his authority, standing, and responsibilities. She knew that, at some point, Owl would become so frustrated that he would fly off on his own. That way, she could continue to play the innocent, while enabling her dear son, Slug, to ease into the CEA's chair. In rare moments of self doubt, she did worry about what he would do there, since she was well aware of his abnormally low intelligence and utter laziness. However, so strong are maternal instincts that they never allowed her to dwell too long on such worries. After all, it would always be she, Stork, who would hold the real reigns of power, allowing the vain Slug to feel important, while ensuring Owl's hard-won efforts on their behalf did not disintegrate in his incompetent hands. This had become even more important in recent days, as Slug had hooked up with a new girlnimal, Flamingo. However, this time, the serial philanderer seemed to be really committed to her, and the relationship looked set to last. On the one hand, Stork was happy that her feckless son had, apparently, found someone to look after him (she was much too cynical to give credence to such nebulous things as love), but on the other, she recognized a fellow gold-digger in Flamingo, and watched her warily.

In many ways, Flamingo could have been Stork's daughter. They looked not dissimilar; both adventurers out to better their fortunes using their gender to best advantage on susceptible partners; both clear-eyed realists, with finely honed self-interest.

Both had managed to ensnare a member of the Forest's ruling animals in their coils. While Stork had, of course, ensured her future by making Panther marry her, a long time ago, Flamingo was still working hard to haul the indecisive Slug to the altar. Stork watched this herculean struggle with some concern, both for her doppelganger (for whom she could not help but have some empathy) as well as for her thoroughly spoilt offspring. The one thing Stork did not find reflected in her potential animal-in-law was the tempered steel of her own soul. Stork's pretty exterior concealed a Machiavellian mind that stopped at absolutely nothing to gain her ends, treading on as many bodies at it took, in the process. She concealed her own slum origins by treating all animals with aggressive arrogance, which she mistook for natural

Authority. She had reeled Panther in skillfully, all those long years ago, till he simply had no escape. This gained her the wealth and social status that she could never have dreamt of in the trashy, frozen marshland she came from. Even though it had meant moving to a distant, tropical Forest from that familiar marshland, she had intuitively understood the necessity of it, if she was ever to rise above her very lowly station in life, despite her lack of education or any natural abilities besides her appearance. Of course, marriage had not deterred Panther's other amorous activities, for he had a major weakness for female animals, and he had offspring in various Forests around the world. Stork was aware of this but grittily chose to ignore it, in her single-minded drive for betterment, knowing she was helpless to prevent it. Under no illusions about her own heritage, she concealed her inner fears and uncertainties from the world, under a harsh facade of haughtiness and pretended superiority. Never having been afflicted with sensitivity of any sort, Stork rode roughshod over every servitor and worker animal that crossed her path, in a crude lurch for power and position – and achieved it. Till Panther's sudden illness, eventually leading to his death, stopped her in her tracks. Now, she was at the mercy of her Son, Slug, and largely shunned by the rest of the animals, most of whom had either suffered at her hands or watched her behavior in horror, from the sidelines, all these many years.

Owl was one of the few animals in the Forest who had seen through her facade to her heaving core of insecurity and fear for her future. Realizing this, and understanding that Owl was too much of a gentleanimal to take advantage of that knowledge, she occasionally let her rigid guard slip with him, providing her with some release from her inner tensions that she so desperately needed. This was one of the major reasons she was never willing to move openly against Owl, even for the advancement of her own Son. The other reason was, of course, her knowledge that Slug was completely incapable of running the warren on his own, without Owl's, or some other experienced animal's, guidance and control. Probably better the known animal than the unknown, she reasoned, uneasily, as she watched the continuing drama, personal and professional, play out.

Stork sighed. She knew that Slug was still completely emotionally dependent on her – something she had carefully nurtured throughout his childhood and young adulthood, with unusual prescience. For the moment, her nest was safe. However, she would have to keep a wary eye on Flamingo. If she weaned Slug too far from his dependence on her, who was to say what could happen. She was shrewd enough to realize that Slug would have no hesitation in turning her out into the wilderness, if he ever realized he did not really need her. She would have to work her charms on Flamingo, she knew, to ensure they both remained dependent on her, which would keep her cozy nest protected. It should not be too difficult, she figured, considering how much they had in common. After all, she had easily ensnared Panther all those years ago, and surely age had not blunted her talons. Anyway, time would tell if her efforts succeeded.

Meanwhile, everyone at the Sanctuary joked that Flamingo was the hardest working animal there – working hard during the day to try and improve the functioning of the warren, and working hard at night to keep Slug thoroughly besotted with her. However, contrary to what Stork believed, she did have enough steel in her soul to push ahead with her plans, with the sort of single-minded determination that made her a mirror image of Stork. At the same time, she recognized herself in Stork and had few illusions about Stork's professed love for her. They needed each other, at least for now – it was a sort of balance of terror, for mutual gain. It made for a somewhat uneasy household, and Flamingo began working very gently on Slug to persuade him to move out of the family nest and into one of their own, at the warren. The warren was, anyway, a far more beautiful place to live in than the old hilltop eyrie which, to her, always felt like a living graveyard. She shivered involuntarily at the thought.

Chapter 9

Owl & Rattlesnake

The three years of building the beautiful warren complex had been perhaps the happiest ones of Owl's long career. He had built up a talented, enthusiastic team of worker and engineer animals, who clearly enjoyed both the work and his leadership, as he mused immodestly. He smiled at the memory of one of his recruits, Dodo, striding from one end of the site to the other, happily singing away, blissfully unaware of the rest of the animals watching him with amusement. In Owl's opinion, it had reflected the true spirit of the warren team and was the prime reason for it being built faster than anything else in the Forest ever had been. The project had become a cause célèbres among the animals of the Forest, and had further cemented Owl's reputation as a leader, especially of Sanctuaries in dire straits. And no straits could be more dire than the one the warren project had been in.

Sadly, those happy days were behind him, he realized at the time. He had not been fooled by Slug, Stork and Flamingo for a moment, and saw clearly through their efforts to covertly undermine him. He had understood that, now the warren complex was complete, their need for him was nearly at an end, and for a family famous for its lack of loyalty to any animal, including their own kin, it would not be long before they wanted his perch.

It was not just Slug's hollow ambitions that annoyed Owl, but, much more, the conduct of Rattlesnake, his chief assistant animal at the warren. Rattlesnake's hypnotic eyes, and alleged mystic visions, had entranced Stork some time ago, and, after much effort, she had finally persuaded Owl to take him on at the warren, as most other Sanctuaries appeared to be actively repulsed by him. For once, Owl's insight had failed him, and he had considered Rattlesnake a desirable and capable addition to his team. Over the ensuing months, he had entrusted him with ever greater responsibility, eventually raising him to the position of de facto second-in-command to himself. Unfortunately, it was in the very nature of Rattlesnake to be sly, cunning and disloyal. While he carefully concealed his intentions from the trusting Owl, he readied the ground to make a grab for the CEA perch from him. While holding Stork securely with his hypnotic lullaby, he worked hard to slowly poison her mind against Owl, with innuendoes and carefully-crafted half insinuations. He was cautious not to accuse Owl of anything specific, as he was well aware of that animal's unassailable reputation and track record. Open, honest battle was, in any case, not Rattlesnake's style. He much preferred the shadowy undergrowth of corporate sanctuary life, the insidious poison in the ear, the hidden fang in the back, the quick rattle sting cloaked in anonymous darkness. It was even better if there was someone else conveniently to hand, to blame the deed upon. The dim-witted and unwary Slug had been heaven-sent for his purposes.

It had not taken Rattlesnake long to have both mother and son mesmerized. And not before time, as Owl's suspicions had gradually begun to awaken about his activities. The first shock that jolted Owl awake to Rattlesnake's real nature was when he discovered that the reptile had inveigled Stork into appointing him to the Board of Director Animals, behind Owl's back. Thereafter, he had noticed a series of seemingly insignificant slights and contrary actions by Rattlesnake as well as a growing tendency for him to take decisions directly to Stork, over Owl's head. It was clearly now only a matter of time for the final push by Rattlesnake. However, Rattlesnake had overestimated Stork's gullibility. While Slug continued to live in his usual waking daze, unaware of most things around him, Stork was far wilier, and had decided that Rattlesnake would suit *her* purposes well, though she was quite unaware of the reptile's own designs. She had decided to use him to undermine Owl, appearing all innocence herself, and then place her son on the CEA's perch. Of course, not for a moment did she consider Rattlesnake for that position. It was the only occasion in his life when that slippery reptile had misjudged a situation, or an animal, and it would cost him dear.

Owl watched the intrigue, and counter-intrigue, swirl around him with sad, dawning understanding. He had never been a political animal in his life, and had zero tolerance for it in anyone working with him. However, for that very reason, he had no understanding of how to counter it, especially when the wand was wielded by masters of that art, like Stork and Rattlesnake. With the straightforward, old Panther now living out his final days, paralyzed beyond any ability to intervene, even if his dying brain did register what was happening at his beloved Sanctuary, a growing sense of frustration and anger engulfed Owl. He knew it would soon be time for him to fly away, while his gravitas and reputation remained untarnished. In a way, it would be poetic justice to leave Stork, Slug and Rattlesnake to deal with each other. It was the team that he really felt for. They were truly wonderful and trusted him implicitly. He knew he would be letting them down, with his departure, but could think of no viable alternative. Despondently, he wondered where he should head to next.

On some days, Owl felt his years weigh heavily on his feathered, grey shoulders. What a strange, wandering life he had led. Not that he regretted it for a moment, as those nomadic voyages had provided him with a plethora of exciting, rewarding and fascinating experiences, and built his reputation to the pinnacle it had now reached, he mused, as usual, somewhat less than modestly. Perhaps he had allowed the growing chorus of praise from the media birds of the Forest to swell his head just a bit! The appreciation of his helpless inadequacy, in the face of Sanctuary intrigue and politics, was just what he needed to bring his feet back down from the air to the hard earth. Anyway, it had been a good run, and he had notched up a major achievement on his oaken pole.

As he sat musing, his Secretarimal, Oryx, galloped in to remind him that he had a Board of Director Animals meeting in a few minutes. The Board was something he had created, to make himself more accountable, though it was not required under the laws of the Forest. Panther and his family had been completely mystified, unable to comprehend why Owl would wish to voluntarily restrict the absolute authority they had given him. Rattlesnake had simply sniggered at Owl's naiveté, quietly setting in motion plans to get himself nominated to this Board by conning Stork, something he knew he could do with the greatest ease. Once there, he would gradually work on each member, to undermine, and eventually replace, Owl as CEA. And, of course, he could keep showing up apparent discord in Owl's team by contradicting him in front of the Asses and, frequently, tabling papers he had taken care to keep Owl ignorant of before the meeting. Fate was being unusually kind to him.

Vaguely aware of these risks, the clear-sighted Owl nevertheless pushed ahead with the creation of the Board, which set a standard of Sanctuary governance that his own sense of ethics and the professionalism that had been honed by his many years at the storied multi-Forest sanctuary, Unihandle, was comfortable with. Since the mortally ill Panther was incapable of heading it, he appointed the respected local Forest-environment expert, Dr. Giraffe, to the Head Perch on the Board and, among others, brought in Donkey as another independent member. Stork viewed these 'independent' appointees complacently as she was well aware that she could easily ride roughshod over them, should she choose to do so. Rattlesnake, too, was confident in his own deviousness and knew he could either corrupt them or undermine them, as required, to gain his own ends. Most unusually, he continued to be blind to Stork's designs. However, so far, the Board had functioned well and Owl was quite satisfied, despite Stork's obviously growing restiveness, and Rattlesnake's ominous and unwelcome presence.

As he stood at the mouth of the Board Cave, greeting each Ass as he arrived for the meeting, Donkey drew him aside for a moment. "Owl, my friend, I have been asked to sound you out on a very confidential matter. As you know, I am CEA of the most important government Sanctuary in this Forest, and we have just been given a huge, exciting project to build beach bird-baths. It was originally planned by a foreign sanctuary but their resources failed them and they collapsed, quite spectacularly. The biggest venture King Lion has ever entrusted to us, it could have far-reaching implications for all the animals in our Forest. Naturally, my boss, Minister Ostrich, is very nervous and insists on my finding a really capable animal to run it. In fact, he suggested your name, and asked me to see if you would consider taking it on. It would mean you would be working under me, but, as we are friends, and as my Sanctuary is many times bigger than this one, I feel you would be quite comfortable. And, of course, I would give you absolute freedom to run the project the way you wish. Would you consider it?"

Owl was stunned by the unexpectedness of the offer, and not a little pleased that it should have come from Minister Ostrich himself. Flummoxed for a moment, he pleaded with his friend for a bit of time to take it all in and think it through. Smiling broadly, Donkey told him that he had the entire duration of the meeting to think it over! One deep in thought, and the other smiling his usual Colgate smile, they walked into the Board Cave. If only Owl had realized then how his friend would betray him in the years to come.

It had not taken Owl long to make up his mind. Not only was the opportunity a huge one, which could put the final cherry on his growing name and fame, his ever-susceptible ego could not but be flattered by the fact that Minister Ostrich had asked for him specifically. And, of course, the situation in his beloved warren, the warren he had unstintingly poured his entire heart and soul into, was rapidly deteriorating, to an extent that was becoming unacceptable to an animal of his integrity and morals.

Thus it came to pass that, one gloomy, overcast day, Owl eventually did take wing and fly away from the warren, off to Donkey's Sanctuary and what, he prayed, would be an opportunity to create something wonderful for the animals of the Forest, without interference, intrigue or politicking. He left the sleazy crowd of Rattlesnake, Stork, Slug and Flamingo with no regret. However, he could not prevent himself from flying one final salute, high in the air over his beloved warren, as he bid it farewell with an overflowing heart, and headed into the western sky, never to return.

Chapter 10

Owl, Bear Cub, Jackal & Skunk

A desperate scratching at the base of the tree, on which he perched, jerked Owl out of his reverie. "Sir, Owl! Sir, Owl! Are you asleep in the middle of the day? I have been calling you for a long time. Please wake up and listen to me," pleaded the desperate voice of Engineer Bear Cub.

"I am sorry, Bear Cub, I was far, far away in my thoughts," apologized Owl, "What is the matter?"

"Jackal is trying to abduct me! I have been running around the Forest, hiding from him, the whole afternoon. He claims you have given me over to him, and that I am now his to do with as he wishes," wept the panicked Bear Cub.

"It's okay, Bear Cub. Relax. It is true that you have been loaned to Jackal, strictly temporarily, on the direct orders of the CEA. However, it is only for a short period and Jackal can only use you to help him out on a specific part of his little animal hotel project. You know how ignorant he is of any real engineering, and I can see he needs someone like you, desperately. So, don't worry. You will be fine with him, for the short time you are there, and I will snatch you back the moment Minister Ostrich gives us the green signal for our beach bird-baths."

"But that has already taken so long! What if he does not decide for many months yet? I don't want to work for Jackal for a day longer than I absolutely must. I understand the CEA has ordered it, but I loathe Jackal. I joined this Sanctuary to work for you, certainly not for Jackal," wailed Bear Cub.

"Rest assured, Bear Cub, I shall keep my eye on you, and I will not let Jackal have you for a day more than I have to. Meanwhile, as you know, the CEA is the CEA and we must all obey his orders – however reluctantly," soothed Owl.

"Once he has his hooks into me, do you really think he will ever let me go?" squeaked Bear Cub, with rare insight.

"I promise I will force our CEA to make him give you up, just as soon as our project is approved," promised Owl, blissfully unaware of the stormy days ahead of him, "In fact, I will make it a condition of my continued handling of the project".

Bear Cub looked miserably at him for a while, but realized that there was not much Owl could really do about the situation. He trusted Owl completely and if Owl said he would be fine for a short time with Jackal, he was willing to reluctantly accept it. Disconsolately, he trundled off in search of the detested Jackal. Sometimes, life was just not fair, he grumbled to himself.

Unknown to them, Jackal was hidden in his favorite underbrush, listening to their conversation. As he watched Bear Cub wander unhappily away, he grinned wickedly, and promised himself a treat, piling up every thankless task on Bear Cub's little shoulders, till he wept. Having indulged himself, he brought his mind back to the threat in Owl's last comment. So, he thought he could turn Donkey against him, Jackal, did he? He would just have to see about that – though, having been bested in his most recent encounter with Owl, he determined to plot his counter-attack with greater care and anticipation. It would have to be a subtle plan. Unfortunately, subtlety was not Jackal's strong suit. He wondered if Peacock could come up with something, though he did not hold out great hopes of anything useful from that vainglorious creature. Did he always have to do all the heavy lifting himself, he fumed silently, as he slunk softly away from Owl's perch.

Jackal was not the only one hiding in the shadows. A pair of very dark, beady eyes coolly regarded all the participants of this drama, as Skunk went about his usual function as a corporate spy. Being aware of his unique fragrance, he ensured he remained at a safe distance, not to give himself away. As both his eyes and ears were equally sharp, this did not place him at any disadvantage. Several senior animals had their envious eyes on Owl's turf, and Skunk was one of them, though he took pains to conceal his ambitions from Donkey. Unlike his perfume, Skunk's mind was quite subtle.

From the beginning, Skunk had felt his personal style cramped by Owl, especially as Owl was able to interact with Donkey directly, as a friend. This did not suit Skunk at all, as he much preferred to be the filter through which everyone had to approach the CEA. Well aware that information is power, he strove hard to be the depository, as well as controller, of all information flowing to or from the CEA. He had already convinced Donkey to allow him to open and sift through all his correspondence, before passing it to him, on the grounds of saving him time and effort – always music to Donkey's ears. The only animals he felt uneasy about were Jackal and Owl. In Jackal, he recognized an even more dangerous predator and had, more or less, resigned himself to accepting him. He even wondered if there was some way he could form an alliance with him. He would need to apply his fertile mind to that problem/opportunity, at leisure.

Owl was another matter. Skunk was shrewd enough to realize that he could not mount a frontal assault on Owl, because of his friendship with Donkey as well as his sterling reputation generally. So, he would need to be 'dealt with' in some other manner. Perhaps, a 'kick upstairs', in some manner, giving him show in place of substance? Somehow he did not think that would really work with Owl. Ideally, Skunk needed him removed from the Sanctuary altogether.

Suddenly, his beady eyes lit up! It was another brilliant idea that could only come from him – even if Skunk was the only one in the Sanctuary who thought of his ideas as brilliant. Was it not just yesterday that he was telling Donkey about the vacancy that had arisen for a CEA in their joint venture with Apep? Now, everyone knew of Apep's terrible professional reputation and disgusting personal lifestyle. No CEA every lasted more than a year or two with him, and the utter mess at his projects were the laughingstock of the

Forest. No sensible animal was willing to work there. However, if Donkey were to "second" Owl there as the new CEA, Owl would have no choice but to accept. And, being a joint venture partner, Donkey had every right to nominate a CEA. Besides, even Apep must surely realize, by now, that no one would willingly work for him and his henchanimals. The icing on the cake would be, if Apep ran true to form, Owl would leave that Sanctuary in disgust in a year or two, and that would be that. They would have got rid of the pesky Owl without, in any way, dirtying their hands. After all, they would ostensibly be handing Owl a huge opportunity, to head up such a massive project, a challenge, they knew, he would genuinely relish.

Skunk excitedly mulled the idea over, as he rambled on through the trees. He knew he would have to handle it very carefully with Donkey, so as not to excite Donkey's own greed for that apparently more powerful perch, or his suspicions of Skunk's motives. Fortunately, he had already dropped the germ of information into Donkey's ear yesterday. Now, like a skillful gardener, he simply had to, gently, nurture the idea into full bloom. Eventually, it would become Donkey's own, original idea! Skunk happily congratulated himself on his own cleverness, and exuded an extra burst of perfume around him, in celebration.

Chapter 11

Forest Fire

At the other end of the Forest, the day had just turned darker for Jackal, *much* darker. The unheard-of had actually happened. The wretched Forest Audit team had descended suddenly on one of his only two animal hotel projects, and in the course of their terrifying rummage, had unearthed a horrendous error that both he and the great Peacock had completely failed to spot. He cursed Peacock and cursed himself. How could they possibly have overlooked something so utterly obvious that even Chartered Animals were able to spot it instantly? It was a basic and self-evident requirement that every animal hotel is planned with a separate set of burrows for the hotel operations animals to live in – something that is blindingly obvious and unchanging. Peacock, despite his loud claims of having built such animal hotels by the hundreds all over the Forests of the world, had completely forgotten to include these in his latest design. While this was a stunning blunder, it was made worse by the fact that Jackal, who always claimed, equally loudly, that he was one of the most experienced builders in the Forest, had not even noticed this glaring omission, and had pushed ahead with building the two animal hotels.

Now, with the animal hotels almost ready to open, one of the two would, unfortunately, have to be used to house the worker animals instead of guest animals, something unheard of in the annals of animal hotel building in any forest in the world. These wretched Forest Audit animals had immediately noticed this huge mess up and gone to town on it. Jackal gnashed his teeth in helpless fury. His anger was mixed with real fear as well. When Donkey heard of this, there would be a price for him to pay, and, who knew, but word might even reach King Lion of this incredible disaster. Jackal shut his eyes in agony, to try and blot out that, worst of all possibilities. A furious King Lion, he knew, would not hesitate to have him for a pre-lunch snack. Equally, he appreciated that Donkey valued his own hide far too much to try and protect Jackal from such danger, even if he wanted to. If that was not bad enough, such news always spread like wildfire in the Forest, and he would soon be reduced to a laughingstock. Jackal's ego just could not bear such a blow. He thrashed about the undergrowth, venting his impotent rage.

Just then, an ashen-faced Peacock skipped in and stopped abruptly at the sight of the half-crazed Jackal. Faced with his furious stare, Peacock stuttered, "Well, it wasn't just my fault! You did not notice it either. I can't do the thinking for everyone, can I? I have so much work on my hands, and Donkey still feels my division has too many architect animals in it! It was just a problem waiting to happen. Anyway, I don't understand what the big deal is. So, we forgot the worker animals' burrows. We will simply build them now. The second animal hotel can be used for guest animals in just two or three years. And what do two or three years matter in a government project?" Peacock tried to brazen it out.

"How dare you try to implicate me in your stupidity, Peacock!" roared Jackal, "How dare you! It is you who is responsible for designing these awful things. I am simply supposed to build what you design, and that is just what I have done. It's not *my* fault if you goof up, you incompetent imbecile! I have a good mind to eat you up whole, here and now."

Despite being badly frightened by Jackal's fury, Peacock was affronted, and managed to quaver, "You won't be able to pass the buck that easily, with the Forest Audit vultures hovering over you. Just wait and see if they pin the blame solely on me! And it does no good to call me names, you know. I would have you remember that I hold certain papers in a certain Snowy Mountains Forest, which would become public, should I happen to suddenly disappear mysteriously. So, just hold your tongue! With the situation as dangerous as it is, we can only survive by sticking together."

The perils of the situation had forced the usually wimpy Peacock to take a desperately more courageous stand with his erstwhile co-conspirator, and it had the desired effect, halting Jackal in his tracks. Whatever else he was, Jackal was no fool, and he knew Peacock held the winning card.

Soothingly he murmured, "I am sorry for my rudeness, my dear old friend. I am sure you understand what a terrible strain this has been on me. Just when everything was going so smoothly, these horrible vultures turn up and unearth something that I know they are going to blow up out of all proportions. After all, as you correctly say, my dear friend, what is the big deal, really? Anyone could have made a small mistake like this. Yes, we both overlooked this little detail. But who can blame us, amidst the thousand and one jobs we are burdened with? If anyone is to blame, I believe it is Donkey, for not giving us enough animals to carry the huge burdens he keeps imposing on us. Don't you agree, my dear Peacock?"

Easily mollified, Peacock agreed, "Yes, without a doubt, the fault is Donkey's, and we must convince the Forest Audit vultures of that."

Jackal went on, warmly, "In fact, it was only yesterday, that I asked him to let me take over Owl's entire division, where all those valuable resources are completely wasted, and he brayed and hawed. Why can't he be a decisive CEA for once? And why is he so frightened of Owl? He is just an old, feathered windbag, anyway. I think Donkey suspected me of wanting to actually swallow that huge beach bird-bath project. Now, Peacock, you know me. Do you think I am capable of such a sneaky, underhand thing? All I wanted was a few more engineer animals and Owl's are sitting around idle."

Peacock suppressed an incredulous smirk, and replied, innocently, "You? Sneaky and underhand? What an idea!"

Jackal looked at Peacock suspiciously, not quite sure if he was being mocked.

"Anyway, Jackal old soul, you might want to be just a bit careful about asking Donkey for additional resources. I know he is a fool, but occasionally he can be quite canny. If he suddenly takes it into his head to check the work being done by our own engineer animals, you know he will find many idle, in both our divisions. We agreed to join forces and build the largest political empire within this Sanctuary. We have to do that very cannily, so as not to arouse anyone's suspicions. Come, we both know you are eager to swallow Owl and his division, and, believe me, I am solidly behind you in that endeavor, but we have to be cautious as Owl is a very experienced, tried and tested old bird, whatever we may say," went on Peacock.

"Ah, he is just an old has-been who has seen better days. So what if he has more real experience and knowledge than the two of us combined? He cannot match your ability to manipulate Donkey, nor my connections with the Asses and other movers and shakers. His project is never going to happen and there is nothing he can do about it. I *shall* have him for lunch – just you wait and watch, my friend," growled Jackal darkly.

"I'm always behind you, as you know. Where you lead, I follow, fearless leader. Only, don't try to throw *me* under the claws of the Forest Audit vultures. We have to stick together on this, as on everything else," said Peacock flatly.

"I wish you were not always *behind* me, but in front of me once in a while," muttered Jackal to himself, walking away.

Peacock looked after him pensively, for a while. His ulcers were playing up again and he had a sour taste in his mouth. Every instinct told him that a storm was brewing, a really big storm, and if he did not find a secure shelter quickly, he would become history. He had no illusions about Jackal's willingness to protect him, beyond the point of mutual self-interest. In fact, it suddenly occurred to him, in a blinding flash, it might even serve Jackal's purpose better if Peacock were to be swept away altogether, in that storm. Then, there would be no blackmailing documents to worry about and the not-so-little nest egg in the Snowy Mountains Forest would become all his, with the passing of his co-conspirator. Blackmail could be a dangerously double-edged sword, he realized. Peacock shivered involuntarily.

It was a whole week before Jackal dared approach Donkey, very tentatively. He and Peacock had hidden out in a remote corner of the Forest, well beyond the reach of the many messengers Donkey had sent out to look for them. Cannily, they had waited for Donkey's annoyance to cool, before putting in an appearance. Knowing his generally sunny and easy-going nature, they knew his fury could not last out the week.

"Where have you been, Jackal, Peacock? I have been looking for you for days!" burst out Donkey, as soon as he saw them peeping furtively around the corner of his lair.

"Ah, Donkey, you can't imagine how hard we have been working on all your many projects. You know we have such an inexperienced group of worker animals that Peacock and I have to do everything ourselves, to teach them. And, we are so short of engineer animals and flying carpets anyway. We are both weary to our very bones," replied Jackal, looking exhausted. He quickly trod on Peacock's claw, to remind him to look equally harassed, tired and unhappy. Since he put this mask on frequently, it was the work of a second for Peacock.

"But you never responded to any of my messages," began Donkey, a little defensively now, "I have been looking for you both to ask you about this damning report the Forest Audit vultures have turned in. Have you really made such a huge blunder?"

"Donkey, my dear old friend, you have known me since childhood. Do you believe me capable of such a mistake? Or even someone with Peacock's years and years and years of animal hotel building experience? Come on! You know what these vultures are like. They hook on to any meat they can get, however rotten or inconsequential, and make a meal of it. You didn't seriously think we had blundered, did you now?" asked Jackal sweetly.

"But they say you are both responsible for this terrible oversight, which will have untold costs over many years," wavered Donkey uncertainly. He was never a clear thinking or decisive animal at the best of times, and an explosion on this scale was enough to completely unanimal him. Even Peacock looked at Jackal a little anxiously, wondering how he could possibly weasel them out of the jaws of doom looming over them.

"Come now, Donkey, as CEA you need to see everything in the correct perspective, not get carried away by their silly hyperbole. After all, this is not the first Forest Audit you have experienced, is it? Here are the facts. It's no big deal, really. One of the junior engineer animals in Peacock's department forgot to include the worker animals' burrows in the design, and one of my new trainee animals, who was responsible for checking it before construction, did not notice it either. As you know, we are both strict disciplinarians, and so we made a barbeque of them both, which the animals of the two departments enjoyed eating. Of course, it serves as a clear lesson to all our worker animals," said Jackal.

Donkey grimaced. Jackal's so-called disciplinary methods always turned his stomach – in some ways, he had not changed at all since their shared childhood, when his favorite games involved stomping the most number of worker ants, or setting fire to the hanging tails of the monkeys sitting up in the branches. Sometimes, he wondered what they really had in common, to bind them to each other.

"Anyway, Peacock discovered this small mistake long before the vultures did, and we have already taken action to sort it out. It will be no problem using the second animal hotel for the worker animal housing, till theirs is built. Work has already begun on that, and it won't be long before it is done. All a big fuss over nothing. We explained it all to the vultures, but these wretched creatures thrive on making mountains of molehills. You remember how they made such a fuss over Peacock's travels, which are so essential. And oh, of course, about your own holding all authority solely in your own hands, contrary to acceptable Sanctuary governance norms," he slid in the painful reminder, slyly. Peacock was filled with admiration at the adroit handling of this sticky situation by Jackal.

"Yes, yes ... ahem. No doubt. I knew they must have got the wrong end of the bamboo somehow," murmured Donkey, now in full, hasty retreat. The reminder of the continuing, serious criticism of himself, not only by Forest Audit, but also by all the Board Asses and just about every animal in his Sanctuary, was a hard jolt. As Jackal had cynically calculated, Donkey now hastened off slippery ground, "Right, let us push rapidly on with the worker animals' burrows. We can rely on the incredibly slow pace of government action. By the time the Forest Audit report ever reaches Minister Ostrich, we will have completed the burrows and that will be that."

"You can bet on it, Boss," burst out both Jackal and Peacock, with relief, and made their hasty getaway from his office.

Chapter 12

Owl in the Night

The dark deed was done! After many weeks of patiently, subtly dropping hints and insinuations into Donkey's naive ears, Skunk had finally managed to convince him that he had himself thought up the most brilliant solution to the Owl problem – and Skunk was ever at hand to applaud the sheer genius of Donkey's plans. Yes, the only way to get rid of the pesky Owl without a furor all around would be to seemingly 'kick him upstairs', apparently rewarding him with the helm of a much larger, albeit highly troubled, ship. He was certain Owl would never see through his ploy and would, in fact, be very pleased with the great new opportunity. On further consideration, thought Donkey smugly, he would sweeten the pill even more, by offering to let Owl take his team with him, since he knew how loyal he was to them. Why, even Skunk thought it was a great idea!

With unusual political savvy, Donkey had patiently lobbied both Apep as well as individual Asses on his Board, and convinced them about the desirability of his plan. Possum was one of the few who saw through it and stubbornly refused to comply with Donkey's wishes. However, he was one of just two Asses who opposed it, and, by the time the meeting was held, Donkey comfortably had all the votes he needed. So pleased was he with the outcome, he had been injudicious enough to gloat to Possum's face, in public. It was a slight Possum stored away at the back of his mind, to feed in the fullness of time. Revenge, as the Forest saying went, was a dish best served cold. And Possum was the sort who never forgot, and never forgave. It was perhaps this single ill-advised moment that would, within a couple of years, lead to Donkey's precipitous fall from grace, being booted out, first, from the Board of Director Asses, and then, from the Sanctuary altogether, yielding his place to Jackal, exactly as Owl had repeatedly forewarned Donkey. But those seeds were sown for an unwary, future harvest. Today, Donkey pranced happily out of the meeting, apparently invincible.

Back in his lair, he decided to lose no time in sending Skunk off to summon Owl, cautioning him not to breathe a word to him about these developments. Skunk was immensely pleased with the fructification of what were, after all, his own plans, but was too canny an animal to allow even a hint of it to show on his sly face. Owl down, Jackal to go, he mused to himself, as he scurried off in search of Owl. Now, he could get on with the next phase of his war plans.

In due course, Owl flew silently into Donkey's lair. As always, the latter started at Owl's totally silent arrival, "Oh! You startled me, Owl! Don't do that! Sing a song, or something, as you approach, so I know you are there."

Owl smiled, amused, "Relax, Donkey! It's just a friend, not a predator or a Forest Audit Vulture. You deal with enough of those, in this Sanctuary, anyway," he added darkly.

"Yes, yes. Well, Owl, my dear friend, I have some really splendid news for you" beamed Donkey, having almost convinced himself that this was as true for Owl as it was for him.

"Oh! Have you finally received approval for our beach bird-baths?" enquired Owl skeptically.

"No, no, Owl. It's something much better for you personally and, being your good friend, I am really delighted to be the one to have got it for you," said Donkey, grandly.

"Okaaay. So what is this great news? I can't think of anything other than our approvals that could merit that descriptor."

"You know how much we all respect and admire you, both here at our Sanctuary as well as in the Forest at large. Even the media birds speak so highly of your track-record of achievements. Your capabilities are far greater than your current assignment justifies, and this has been bothering me for quite some time. It is clear to me that we have perhaps been a bit unfair to you, in terms of the work, and, of course, I have been painfully aware of how frustrated you have been by the Asses' continuing delay of our approvals for your project. To make it worse, Minister Ostrich has just made me aware that your project is unlikely to be cleared at all as, apparently, King Lion is considering giving it away to some foreigners, in exchange for a mutual defence treaty of some sort."

"What! When did you learn of this development? Why have you not told me about it? For heaven's sake!" shouted Owl, completely ignoring everything except Donkey's last piece of news.

"I am as upset as you are, Owl. Believe me, I have only just learnt of this, and, I can assure you, I had a thing or two to say to the Minister, despite his being my Boss. I spoke up courageously against this decision, but, as you can understand, if it comes down from King Lion himself, we can only bow meekly before his wishes," pacified Donkey, with imaginary backbone.

"I can understand that. What I cannot believe is that this is a sudden, new development," fumed Owl.

"Anyway, never mind that, Owl, my friend, let me get to the good news. You know I always look out for your interests, and I have just persuaded the Asses to hand over this huge new challenge to you, which, I know, you will absolutely relish," said Donkey, adding confidentially, "In fact, if truth be told, I would really have liked it for myself. I even tactfully sounded out a few people about my chances. Unfortunately, they all felt I was too valuable here, to be spared. So, I thought of you immediately. It really would be a fitting capstone to your illustrious career. Moreover, no one has any doubts that you will be able to handle the challenge with aplomb."

"You have still not told me just what this great opportunity is," said Owl, patiently and without much enthusiasm.

"Oh, silly me! Now, you know the biggest development Sanctuary in this entire Forest, is our joint venture with Apep of the Heaped Stones Forest. As it happens, their CEA has just trotted away after a final fight with Apep, and there is a plumb vacancy there. It is a very powerful position, overseeing a large number of animals on three huge projects, reporting directly to Apep, in the Heaped Stones Forest. I thought it had your name written all over it, and so I have worked hard on persuading both Apep (who, I must tell you, was hesitant at first) as well as our Asses, to second you to that slot. By the way, the only one who was selfish enough to oppose my recommendation was your so-called friend, Possum. However, I have now received the approval of both Apep as well as our Board of Director Animals. Congratulations, my dear CEA Owl!" enthused Donkey, giving him a warm hug.

Owl mulled it over quietly for a while, without comment. He had never been a believer in free lunches and wondered what the catch was. Finally he said, "Donkey, you know me, and we all know Apep's reputation for unethical, disreputable behavior. However great the opportunity, it is extremely unlikely that he and I will get along. You know that. Yes, the projects are interesting, but they have gigantic hurdles facing them. If Apep, as the Chairanimal of the Asses of that Sanctuary, is confrontational, it will be a complete disaster. This hardly seems such a desirable move, to me," worried Owl.

"Yes, Apep does not have the best reputation for integrity or intelligence. But, he is in so much trouble that he has offered an undertaking to both his and our Boards, not to interfere in the operations of the Sanctuary. Remember, he has, so far, averaged a new CEA each year of that Sanctuary's existence, and each exit was because of his own behavior. What is different now is that you will be representing our shareholding and the interests of *this* Forest generally, in that Sanctuary. Besides, you know you will have my own complete and enthusiastic support at all times. I would not worry about Apep - he is tamed. Remember, I tried to get that position for myself. If it was that bad, do you think I would have put my precious neck in a noose?" reasoned Donkey.

"That is certainly something worth considering. If *you* are going to give me your unstinting backing, perhaps it will be possible to keep Apep in check. I don't know, Donkey, something about it still does not feel absolutely right, and I have a nagging apprehension at the back of my mind. On the one hand, if our beach bird-baths are going nowhere, it would certainly be more desirable to move to a position where I can actually do something worthwhile. On the other hand, there is Apep, and he is a huge negative. Quite a dilemma!"

"But hang on, Owl, that is not all. The position pays very well – much more than you make here. And – get this! – you can even take your team with you, if you wish to. Remember, as I said, you would be there, protecting the interests of our Sanctuary's shareholding," gushed Donkey, desperately. He could feel Owl's indecision keenly, and worked hard to try and reel him in. After all his efforts to set up this golden exit for his nemesis, he just could not afford to let Owl slip out of the trap.

Skunk, with his ear glued to the door, which he had intentionally left slightly ajar, also held his breath. This just could *not* go wrong. A lot of planning and effort had gone into setting this trap.

After a moment of pensive reflection, Owl said, "Ah well, the advantages probably outweigh the disadvantages. Anyway, you know I trust you implicitly, as a good friend. If you can really keep Apep in check, this might work. There is no denying that it is a huge opportunity, and, if I can keep my team....well, okay, let's do it. But remember your promises to me personally, Donkey," said Owl, with some lingering uneasiness.

"Yesss!" exulted Donkey, "That is the right decision, Owl. Of course, my word is my bond. You know me. We will all support you in handling Apep. Great! You start there next week. Good luck, Owl!"

Though he had a vague, uneasy premonition, there was no way for Owl to know that, in just a couple of short years, Donkey would sacrifice him to Apep's whims, without a moment's remorse, when he felt Apep's extensive political connections could work to his advantage with Minister Ostrich. Thus would Skunk's entire cunning plan indeed come full circle. Not that it would save Donkey's own hide for long.

Owl looked sadly at Donkey, and said, not unkindly, "A great CEA requires vision and courage. You are young and inexperienced. If, over the years, you manage to acquire both, you have the potential to rise right to the top in this Forest. Why, one day, King Lion could even select you to replace this nincompoop Minister Ostrich. Good luck!" With a shrug, Owl took wing, into the night, towards the tropical storm that had been gathering all evening, at the edges of the Forest.

Tomorrow would see a different dawn.

Disclaimer

So, who am I, who have chronicled the diverse goings-on at these Sanctuaries of ours? I am Owl, the Wakia Nawish, the recorder of events and observer of animals. While this little "corporate frolic" does draw on my own real-life, professional experiences of four decades of working in diverse "Sanctuaries" around the world, it is focused on part of my experiences in the "Mountainous Desert Forest" in the Middle East. While all the experiences are indeed true and many of the personality facets of the animals here are familiar at "Sanctuaries" everywhere, if you think you recognize someone specific, rest assured these particular animals are figments of my mind! So, perhaps it's just your mirror talking?

Much have I seen and heard ....

THE END

www.ingramcontent.com/pod-product-compliance
Lightning Source LLC
LaVergne TN
LVHW020416070526
838199LV00054B/3640
* 9 7 9 8 8 6 9 1 8 7 1 6 1 *